I AM AN INDIAN

I AM AN INDIAN

Edited by Kent Gooderham

J. M. DENT & SONS (CANADA) LIMITED, TORONTO

Copyright © 1969 by
J. M. Dent & Sons (Canada) Limited

Paperback   ISBN   0-460-92552-0
Hardcover   ISBN   0-460-92551-2

Cover

The upper picture on the cover, "Canadian Geese", is by Francis Kagige (Ojibway for "Forever"), a self-taught Odawa Indian from Manitoulin Island, Ontario.

The lower picture on the cover, "Thunderbird Fish", is by Norval Morriseau, whose Indian name is Copper Thunderbird. Mr. Morriseau is an Ojibway, born and raised in the area northwest of Lake Superior.

ACKNOWLEDGMENTS

The editor and the publishers wish to extend grateful acknowledgment to the following for the use of the material quoted.

Howard Adams: "The Haves and Have Nots".

The Arctic Institute of North America and Robert A. McKennan: "Kleviti Defeats the Eskimo" by Johnny Frank, from The Arctic Institute of North America Technical Paper No. 17, "The Chandlar Kutchin" by Robert A. McKennan, September, 1965.

Jackson Beardy: "Wesakachak and the Beaver" and "Wesakachak and the Geese" from *Compiled Indian Legends* by Jackson Beardy.

Lloyd R. Caibaiosai: "The White Yum-Yum Tree", taken from a talk given at Glendon College, York University, Toronto, 1968.

The Canadian Research Center for Anthropology: "The Revenge of the Caribou"

iv

Image Productions: "Ronnie" by Ronald Potts. From the film released by Image Productions, 1968.

Institute of American Indian Arts and Phil George: "Old Man the Sweat Lodge".

Institute of American Indian Arts and Tommy Smith: "Gonna Ride a Bull".

Frances A. (Bazil) Katasse: "Uncertain Admission".

T.R. Kelly: "My People the Haida" by Rev. Dr. Peter Kelly from *The Indians Speak to Canada*, published by the King's Printer, 1939.

The Macmillan Company of Canada Limited: "Tetlaneetsa" and "Wolverine and the Great Serpent" by Marius Barbeau. Adapted from *The Indian Speaks* by Marius Barbeau by permission of the author.

Leonard S. Marchand: "The Honourable Member for Kamloops-Cariboo".

Peter Martin Associates Limited: "Rabbit Hunting" from *A Trapper's Life* by John Tetso, soon to be published by Peter Martin Associates Limited.

McClelland and Stewart Limited: "The Making of the Great Law" from *Indian Legends of Canada* by Ella Elizabeth Clark. Reprinted by permission of The Canadian Publishers, McClelland and Stewart Limited, Toronto. "The Floating Island" from *Indian Legends of Canada* by Ella Elizabeth Clark. Reprinted by permission of The Canadian Publishers, McClelland and Stewart Limited, Toronto.

McGraw-Hill, Inc.: "Handsome Lake", reprinted by permission from *Red Jacket* by Arthur C. Parker. Copyright 1955 by McGraw-Hill, Inc.

J. McLeod: "Conversations with Maria Michano" from *North* (March/April 1968).

Gordon Moore: "The Spell of the Windego" from *Indian News*, December, 1967, published by the Department of Indian Affairs and Northern Development.

The Northian: "The Face of a Thief" by Phil Thompson. Published by the Society for Indian and Northern Education, 1965.

Clarence Oppenheim: "Loss for Progress".

Howard H. Peckam: "Pontiac's War" from *Pontiac and the Indian Uprising* by Howard H. Peckam, Princeton University Press (1947) and University of Chicago Press (1961).

Duke Redbird: "The Beaver". Published by the *Canadian Free Press*, 1968.

Vivian Rowland: "The Spirit Trail".

The Ryerson Press: "My People the Great Ojibway" from *Legends of My People, The Great Ojibway* by Norval Morriseau, edited by Selwyn Dewdney. Reprinted by permission of the Ryerson Press, Toronto.

vi

Saskatchewan History and Folklore Society: "Payepot the Sioux-Cree Chief" from *Payepot and His People* by Abel Watetch as told to Blodwen Davies. Published by the Saskatchewan History and Folklore Society.

Charles Scribner's Sons: "The Race". Reprinted with the permission of Charles Scribner's Sons from *Blackfoot Lodge Tales* by George Bird Grinnell, pages 155 to 156.

Smithsonian Institution: "The Potlatch Song of Qwaxila" from the 35th. Annual Report of the Bureau of American Ethnology (Part 2) by Franz Boas, 1913-14.

Mary Jane Sterling: "Thoughts on Silence".

Saul Terry: "Faces" and "Coming of Age".

Lorna Jamieson Thomas: "The Hideous One".

University of California Press: "Coyote and the Monster of the Columbia" from *Indian Legends of the Pacific Northwest* by Ella E. Clark. Published by the University of California Press, 1960.

University of Nebraska Press: "A Loon I Thought it Was", "The Sky Clears", "I Will Walk", "Now I Am Left", and "Passamaquoddy War Song" from *The Sky Clears* by A. Grove Day. Copyright 1951 by A. Grove Day. Reprinted from the 1964 University of Nebraska Press edition by permission of the publisher.

University of Toronto Press: "On the Death of an Uncle" from *The Iroquois Book of Rites* by Horatio Hale. Published by the University of Toronto Press, 1963.

University of Wisconsin Press: "No Longer the Middle Five" from *The Middle Five* by Francis La Flesche; © 1963 by the Regents of the University of Wisconsin Press.

Gordon Williams: "The Last Crackle".

The Bond Wheelwright Company: "Gluskap and the King of France" and "N'Jacques and Kitty" from *Gluskap the Liar and Other Indian Tales* by Horace P. Beck, 1966.

Yale University Press: "A Cannibal Loose in St. Louis" by Charley Nowell from Clellan S. Ford, *Smoke from Their Fires* (Yale University Press, New Haven, 1941), adapted from pages 186-188.

Photographs

Canadian Wildlife Services: p.185

Department of Citizenship and Immigration: p.46, p.131

Department of Indian Affairs and Northern Development: p.35, p.43, p.46, p.124, p.193

Glenbow Foundation: p.31, p.52, p.57, p.67, p.71, p.82, p.90, p.111

Mrs. Alma Greene: p.174

National Museum of Canada: p.13, p.156, p.166

Public Archives of Canada: p.6, p.11, p.16, p.69, p.72, p.88, p.128, p.159, p.180, p.188

Vancouver Sun: p.18

Whitehorse Star: p.121

Paintings and Drawings

The paintings and drawings on the cover and on p.ii, p.50, p.62, p.75, and p.135 are from the National Collection and are reproduced by permission of the artists and the Cultural Development Section of the Department of Indian Affairs and Northern Development.

The drawing on p.xviii of Ko-ishin-mit is by George Clutesi and is used by permission of Gray's Publishing Ltd., Sidney, British Columbia.

The drawing on p.27 of Coyote and the Monster of the Columbia is by Saul Terry.

The publishers have made every reasonable effort to ensure that these acknowledgments are complete and correct; nevertheless, apology is made for any inadvertent errors or omissions.

Editor's Acknowledgments

That I was able to start *I Am An Indian* at all was due in no small part to the encouragement of such authors as George Clutesi and Howard Adams. Thecla Zeeh, then Editor of *The Northian,* Jean Goodwill of *Indian News,* James McGrath of the Institute of American Indian Arts, Diane Armstrong of *North,* and Dorothy Neville of Indian Affairs not only provided encouragement but introductions to exciting authors as well.

In my efforts to produce a book which might do justice to the Indian people of Canada I relied upon yet another set of friends and experts who read and criticized the manuscript. My wife, Helen, spent hours reading and reacting to an almost endless series of possible selections but kept her cool and battled for the selections she liked best. Dr. G. M. Day of the National Museum, Dr. R. W. Dunning of the Department of Anthropology, University of Toronto, and Hugh Dempsey of the Glenbow Foundation read early versions of the anthology and saved me from making serious errors. So too did Shirley Daniels of the National Museum, John Dockstader, author and artist, and Roy Daniels of the National Film Board who read one of the chapters in the airport in Winnipeg as we waited for our flight to Western Canada. Val Pepin not only gave her candid opinion on each of the possible selections but with the assistance of Ruth Bennett and Mary Ann Dinsdale, typed and retyped each of the versions of the anthology.

Many people helped collect the illustrations: Marion Smythe and Catherine Donnelly of Indian Affairs and Northern Development, Sheilagh Jameson of the Glenbow Foundation, and Mrs. James Whyard of *The Whitehorse Star* were particularly patient and persevering.

Much of the credit for the fact that the anthology has been published must go to Robert F. Davey and Leslie Waller of the Education Branch of Indian Affairs and Northern Development whose support made it possible. But most of all my appreciation goes to the men and women who wrote the material and who agreed to have their work included in *I Am An Indian.* I hope that the final product does credit to all of them and that they will overlook any errors which may appear in the text.

INTRODUCTION

The Indians of Canada are not alike. Separated by language, culture, and geography they are as different from one another as they are from the Europeans, Asians, and Africans who came to live among them. They resemble their movie image even less.

When Christopher Columbus mistook North America for India and called the inhabitants Indians he made an error still not corrected almost five hundred years later. The people whose ancestors have lived on this continent for tens of thousands of years belong to eleven different language groups.

Among the people who speak a similar language there are many tribes. The Blackfoot of the western plains and the Micmac of the Atlantic coast who both speak Algonkian languages live thousands of miles apart and until modern times never met, or knew that the other existed. Even among the tribes there are wide differences. Bands separated for long periods of time developed ways of living so different that they now have little in common other than language.

The variety of experience among Indian people is almost endless — so much so that it may be impossible to write all about Indians or even to represent the many Indian points of view.

This book attempts a brief glimpse into the ever changing living patterns of Indians in Canada. It is a book written by Indians—men and women who are called Indians but think of themselves as Sioux or Salish, Ojibway or Delaware, Abnakis or Assiniboine.

What wonderful names these proud Indian names! Reciting them evokes the richness, the excitement, the diversity they represent. The authors who speak in this book offer some of this wealth. They speak of a world of wars and treaties, honour and treachery, feasts and hunger. They write about people who laugh and people who cry; people to be proud of; teachers to learn from; leaders to follow; heroes to love.

Some who have attended modern schools use English with as much grace as they use their own language. Others have created a language of their own which uses English words in a unique and meaningful way. How the story is told is as important as the story itself and every effort has been made to retain the original wording of the author.

UNCERTAIN ADMISSION

The sky looks down on me in aimless blues
The sun glares at me with a questioning light
The mountains tower over me with uncertain shadows
The trees sway in the bewildered breeze
The deers dance in perplexed rhythms
The ants crawl around me in untrusting circles
The birds soar above me with doubtful dips and dives.
They all, in their own way, ask the question
Who are you, who are you?
I have to admit to them to myself
I am an Indian.

Frances A. (Bazil) Katasse

First Prize under 16 category. Scottsdale National Indian
Arts Exhibition 1965.

CONTENTS

Chapter IX   PEOPLE OF THE SUNRISE   175

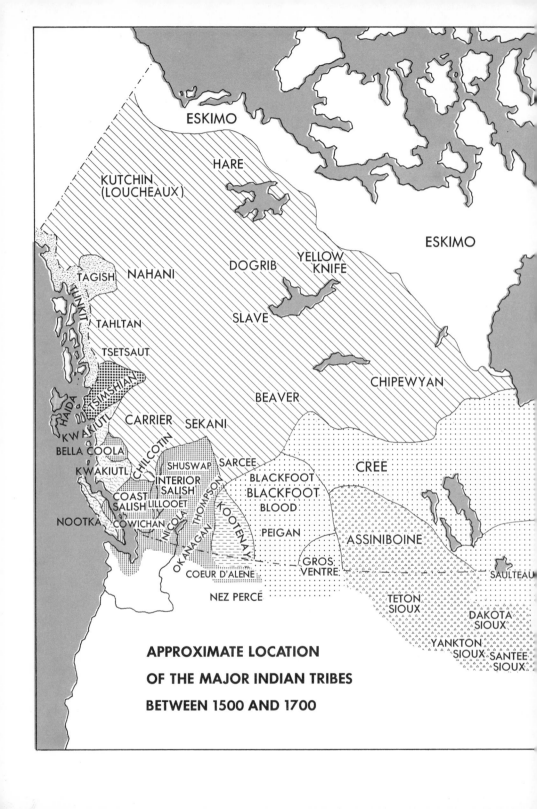

ESKIMO

HARE

KUTCHIN
(LOUCHEAUX)

ESKIMO

TAGISH
NAHANI
DOGRIB
YELLOW
KNIFE

TLINKIT

TAHLTAN
SLAVE

TSETSAUT

CHIPEWYAN

HAIDA
TSIMSHIAN

BEAVER

KWAKIUTL
CARRIER
SEKANI

BELLA COOLA
CHILCOTIN

KWAKIUTL
SHUSWAP
SARCEE

CREE

INTERIOR
SALISH
BLACKFOOT

COAST
SALISH
LILLOOET
BLACKFOOT

NOOTKA
COWICHAN
NICOLA
THOMPSON
BLOOD

OKANAGAN
KOOTENAY
PEIGAN
ASSINIBOINE

GROS
VENTRE
SAULTEAU

COEUR D'ALENE

NEZ PERCÉ
TETON
SIOUX

DAKOTA
SIOUX

APPROXIMATE LOCATION
YANKTON
SIOUX
SANTEE

OF THE MAJOR INDIAN TRIBES
SIOUX

BETWEEN 1500 AND 1700

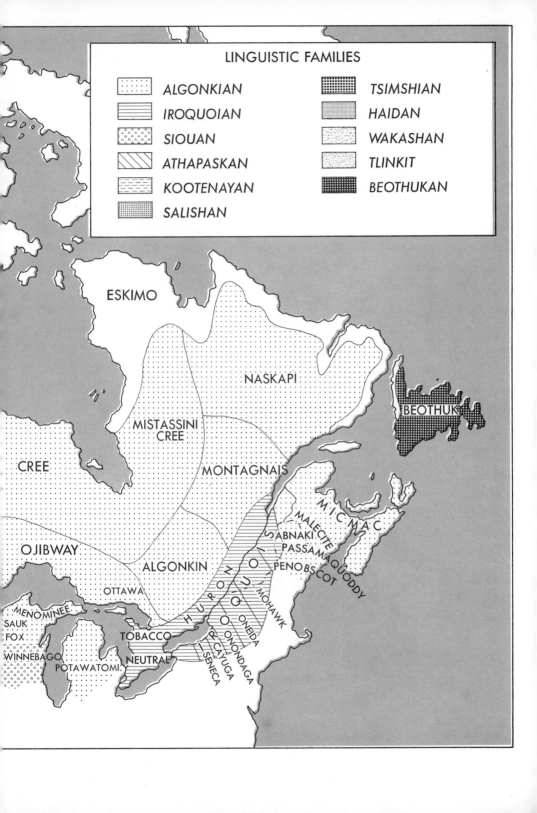

LINGUISTIC FAMILIES

ALGONKIAN		TSIMSHIAN	
IROQUOIAN		HAIDAN	
SIOUAN		WAKASHAN	
ATHAPASKAN		TLINKIT	
KOOTENAYAN		BEOTHUKAN	
SALISHAN			

ESKIMO

NASKAPI

BEOTHUK

MISTASSINI
CREE

CREE

MONTAGNAIS

MICMAC

MALECITE

ABNAKI

PASSAMAQUODDY

OJIBWAY

PENOBSCOT

ALGONKIN

OTTAWA

HURON

MOHAWK

MENOMINEE

SAUK

FOX

TOBACCO

ONEIDA

WINNEBAGO

NEUTRAL

ONONDAGA

POTAWATOMI

CAYUGA

SENECA

Ko-ishin-mit by George Clutesi

Chapter I

Artists and Aristocrats

Where the forests meet the surf, the people — the Haida, Tsimshian, Kwakiutl, Bella Coola, Nootka, and Salish — built their homes, huge cedar buildings adorned with majestic heraldic designs.

From the sea, the pounding Pacific, the bays, fiords, and sounds, and from the roaring coastal rivers, they took the salmon as well as a multitude of "lesser" fish. In the forest they found the cedar from which they built their homes and their boats, wove their clothing, and carved the mighty totem poles for which they are famous throughout the world.

Hereditary rights, guarded by an aristocracy, were expanded through a series of power plays known as potlatches — huge parties held by chiefs at which guests were invited to feast, dance, receive gifts, and witness the power of their host.

The Haida built cedar canoes that carried one hundred men with all their gear. The Tsimshian built the tallest totems in the world. The Nootka fought and conquered the whale. The Kwakiutl and Bella Coola invented societies that staged dances, songs, and ceremonies that ran for weeks at a time. The baskets, robes, and blankets of the Salish were unsurpassed and today no sportsman is happy until he owns a Cowichan sweater.

The coast people were travellers ready to go great distances to get what they wanted, whether it was slaves or candlefish oil. They travel today too, for education, for employment, and for the joy of experiencing the unknown. There are few families on the west coast of British Columbia who cannot point to relatives who have made good in faraway places.

KO-ISHIN-MIT TAKES A PARTNER

The stories of Ko-ishin-mit, the Son of Raven, and his friends have been told by members of the Clutesi family for hundreds of years. This fable of the Tse-shaht people, who were allies of the Nootka, is told by George Clutesi. Mr. Clutesi is a very versatile man. He is a painter, poet, teacher, and lecturer. His talents are well known throughout British Columbia and particularly in Vancouver Island where he studied under the famous artist, Emily Carr. She was so impressed with his ability that she willed him her brushes and oils. Her faith was not misplaced. In 1966 Clutesi was commissioned to paint one of the major external murals on the Indians of Canada Pavilion at Expo 67.

It was a fine sunny morning. Ko-ishin-mit was out as usual, his keen nose sniffing for a possible source of a free meal. He had a very sharp, keen sense of smell. He could detect the smell of cooking from a great distance and he could go straight to the source of the cooking aroma.

Son of Shag and Son of Saw-bill were sunning themselves in front of the village when Ko-ishin-mit came ambling along with his nose in the air. He was following the smell of cooking salmon that had drifted down on the morning breeze. He could hear the two men talking. They seemed to be discussing something of grave importance because they were speaking earnestly. Suddenly Ko-ishin-mit heard his own name mentioned and he slackened his pace and listened more intently.

"Son of Saw-bill listen to me. It is a shame that a man of such noble birth, a man of such distinction, a man so important, should go about without a man-servant and bodyguard. All men of high birth should have servants. I say that Ko-ishin-mit should, by his own rights as a man of noble birth, appoint a man-servant and bodyguard right now. It is beneath his dignity to go about without a man-servant." Son of Shag spoke loud enough so that Ko-ishin-mit would hear every word that he said. Both men knew how conceited the Son of Raven was.

Ko-ishin-mit did not stop to hear more. Instead he quickened his pace. The two plotters saw Ko-ishin-mit strut more proudly. He raised his nose higher. He stopped following the aroma of cooking salmon.

"Look now, Son of Saw-bill, the greedy one is actually passing up a meal. He's up to something. He heard every word said about him. Ko-ishin-mit likes his free meals too well to pass one up. He's thinking of something better than a meal for himself, you can rely on that," Son of Shag declared. Both men chuckled with glee as Ko-ishin-mit hurried past all the houses.

Ko-ishin-mit was thinking. He was a crafty, cunning person. He had always boasted that he could think for himself and this was one of the times, he boasted to himself, as he hurried back to his little house.

"If I have a man-servant he would have to go with me on my social calls and my host would have to feed him also. This would mean I would have that much less to eat. That would never do. On the other hand, as the wise Son of Shag has stated, it is beneath my dignity as one of noble birth to go without a man-servant. Yes, I must get a man-servant — but one that doesn't eat too much, I think," he mused.

The tide was out. The slender sea-grass and the delicate seaweed waved and beckoned in the shallow pools along the seashore. A tiny little house stood on the very edge of the sea just above high-water mark. It was a very pretty little house and Ko-ishin-mit approached it with a deliberate step. He did not hurry, neither did he tarry. Straight to the little house he went.

As he drew near, the smallest person imaginable appeared in the little doorway. He was obviously a happy little man for his red, rotund cheeks were wreathed in smiles. He was the Son of Sea Urchin, a member of the [tribe of the] smallest people in the world.

"Come in, Ko-ishin-mit. May I offer you a nice feed of dried sea-weed?" he chortled in his weak little voice.

Ko-ishin-mit did not like dried seaweed, but he could not resist an offer of free food so he ate it. Ko-ishin-mit was always polite so he thanked Son of Sea Urchin for the seaweed.

"Hear me now, Son of Sea Urchin. I, Son of Raven, have come to offer you a great honour," he stated slowly and deliberately. "I have given this much thought and this day, Son of Sea Urchin, I have chosen you to be my companion and partner. Your duties will be light. You will be required to accompany me on my social calls. Now know this.

It will be a great honour to you. Until now I have not permitted anyone to associate with my personage. What say you, Son of Sea Urchin, will you consent to be my partner?" The proud young Raven spoke in a loud, commanding voice. He was at his very most arrogant self.

The little man thought the offer over for a short time and then he answered, "Son of Raven, I shall be very happy to be your companion. Yes, I shall be your partner," he said in his very small voice.

On their first social call they were served fresh salmon roasted over an open fire. Each was given an equal helping of the delicious food and Ko-ishin-mit, as was his wont, gulped his portion down as quickly as he could, so he could perhaps have more. Son of Sea Urchin placed a small piece in his tiny mouth and began to chew it, taking much time and showing good manners. The Raven ogled his companion's share of the food with greedy, bulging eyes.

"Nah, my partner, you have far too much on your platter. Remember you are a very small person," Ko-ishin-mit pointed out. "Indeed I shall be very happy to help you eat some of your share," he slyly wheedled. Before the tiny man could reply, greedy Ko-ishin-mit reached across and began gobbling his partner's dinner. He ate and he ate, in fact he ate so much that he became ill and had to be carried to his home.

It was a strange procession. They had put the Raven on a cedar slab and the host had taken the head of the stretcher while the tiny Son of Sea Urchin did his best to hold up the foot of the wide board. The weight of the bloated Ko-ishin-mit was far too much for the little man and he began to choke on the very first mouthful he had been able to get before the Raven had grabbed his food. At last, they managed to get the bloated Ko-ishin-mit to his home where long-suffering Pash-hook [his wife] took charge and put him to bed.

Ko-ishin-mit opened his beady little eyes and the very first thing he saw was his man-servant still chewing on the first mouthful of salmon. He propped himself on his elbow and groaned.

"Do not be such a glutton, Son of Sea Urchin," he roared, "shame on you. You are still eating. The next time I take you out on my social calls I shall have to take all your share."

George Clutesi

A CANNIBAL LOOSE IN ST. LOUIS

One of the most important of the Kwakiutl secret societies is the Hamatsa or Cannibal Society. This group occasionally puts on performances of a magical dance designed to scare the audience.

A member makes some mistake in the dance and appears to become furious. This enraged cannibal rushes wildly about, seizes and kills a victim before the eyes of his horrified audience.

In this story Charles James Nowell, the Kwakiutl chief, describes the dance he and his Hamatsa partner, Bob Harris, performed at the 1904 St. Louis Fair in front of thousands of spectators.

There is a good story about our dance at St. Louis. We were given notice about a week beforehand that very important people were going to come to see us. So we got everything ready — our dancing blankets, and a headdress with ermine skins on the back, and Bob Harris made everything ready for himself, because he was a Hamatsa (member of the Cannibal Society).

There was a little African pygmy that used to come and see us. He liked to come because we always had bananas, and this little fellow loved bananas. He didn't seem to want to eat anything else; as soon as he came in, he looked at the bananas hanging up and said, "Huh — Banana!"

Bob Harris wanted to make a little man just like him, so I told the pygmy to come in every day and sit down and eat bananas while Bob Harris was making a likeness of him with some bones and mutton flesh. He made it just like him, and when it was finished it was put in an oven, and Bob Harris looked after it while it was baking. Bob Harris took it out and held it up alongside of the little man, and the little fellow would offer it a banana. Bob Harris was making a whistle; he pinched the little fellow to make him squawk, until he was able to make a whistle that sounded just like him. He made the mouth of this thing to move, and he put the whistle under the skirt of the little likeness he made, so that every time he pressed where the whistle was, it made the right noise. He filled the inside with a tube of blood.

We went to the place where all the people were. There were about twenty thousand people that came that time. We had a screen that was painted in a square — about eight feet square. We told the little fellow how it was going to be done, and not to tell his friends about it or we wouldn't give him any more bananas. We had this baked-mutton man inside the screen, where all our dresses were.

We began with a Bella Bella dance; the West Coast people all knew the songs, and they were singing while Bob Harris and I were dancing. When we got nearly through one song, Bob Harris made a mistake in beating, and then he said, "Hap-hap-hap." I got behind the screen and dressed as an Indian and came back and told the people in English that the Cannibal is mad now, because he made a mistake in beating the board, and we don't know what he is going to do, because he is so fierce.

Two young men from the West Coast came and held him—trying to keep him from going toward the other people. Bob Harris was struggling to get free from their hold. Finally he got away from them, and he ran around. When he got to where this little pygmy was sitting, he picked him up and ran behind the screen and left him there. Then he took hold of this likeness and made it squeak and yell, and when he came out in front of the screen, it was yelling loud. Bob Harris came

Masked Kwakiutl dancers.

in front of us and set this little fellow in front of us and pushed his head down and bit the neck until out came the blood all over his face. All the little pygmies got up with their spears and were coming to kill Bob, and all the people in the audience thought sure he had bitten the pygmy's neck off, but the guards just pushed them back and told them to sit down. The little pygmies just went home while Bob Harris was eating the mutton. I was the one that was cutting the flesh in strips while he was eating them, and crying, "Hap-hap". When he got through eating — some of us helped him because we were hungry — I looked around and saw there was no Indian in that place; they had all got frightened and gone home.

Charles James Nowell

LAUGHTER BEHIND THE TREES

Early Europeans observing the Tloo-qwah-nah heard the Nootka verb Pa-chitle, to give, over and over. Misunderstanding the significance of the word they thought the name of the ceremony was Potlatch.

When George Clutesi was a young man he attended the last Tloo-qwah-nah or Potlatch held by the Nootka people. At that time the Potlatch had been declared illegal and one of his relatives was arrested for sponsoring the festival.

Mr. Clutesi, a courageous as well as a talented man, has decided that it is time Canadians heard the Indians' point of view. In his book Potlatch *he describes what actually happened in that most spectacular celebration which lasted a full twenty-eight days.*

Each of the many dances in the Tloo-qwah-nah rivalled its prede-cessor in grace, imagination, and drama but one of the most beautiful was "Laughter Behind the Trees".

Each and every participant of the Tloo-qwah-nah would start his own ceremony by rendering his own incantation, songs and plays in accor-dance with their importance. The more important ones were always reserved for the end of the event.

During the initial period of the Tloo-qwah-nah proper many songs were sung, many dances and plays performed. The days sped by as the feasts increased in number. One family after another rose to an-nounce their intention to join, to participate, because their hearts had been reached — moved by the songs and the rituals. There was never a slow or a dull moment during the entire Tloo-qwah-nah. The plays that were shown were varied, educational and full of interest, partic-ularly to the younger men and women for whose benefit they were performed.

One of them occurred with no announcement whatever except, per-haps, that the four great fires were allowed to wane low on their hearths.

Haaaah ha ha ha ha ha. Haaaah ha ha ha ha ha.

A peal of feminine laughter issued forth from the shadows outside the great doors of the lodge as a comely young woman darted in, then darted hither and yon seeking the shadows, to be followed immediately by a second, a third and yet another until there were seven in all. Dart-ing behind screens and behind round posts that had been placed the night before, ostensibly to support the huge beams, they let out peals of sensual laughter as they gained the shadows. The young women never showed themselves other than by provocative darts from one shadow to another. No laugh was heard individually, it issued forth from seven directions almost simultaneously. Each player darted behind the posts towards the place of the fires to keep out of sight of the onlookers, and behind other screens that were placed conveniently between the posts. The four fires were waning low on their hearths, the narrow smoke-holes were closed to narrow slits, blue smoke permeated the already darkened atmosphere inside the great lodge.

The performers were dressed in long flowing robes made from the inner bark of the yellow cedar; some in its natural white, some dyed red or a disturbing orange. The girls' deep-set eyes were shadowed black to and beyond their cheekbones. There was a dash of red ochre upon each cheek and their brows were arched and pencilled black to allure the young and unwary. They made no move or approach to the men, or to anyone, as they darted from one shadow to the other behind posts and screens while they sent forth disarming laughter from their concealment. The darting women made the entire round of the planted posts, never showing themselves between each seductive move, but the peals of provocative laughter never ceased. They laughed themselves out of the arena as they had come in.

Haaaah ha ha ha ha ha.

"We have seen, you and I, the laughing sirens of the trees. We have been fortunate because, it is said, they are rarely seen, if ever, that they never venture beyond the forest of pine and cedar but stay in the shadows of the thicket of the wood. It is said that these women you have seen cannot think for themselves, that their minds are not their own. It is said that the women you have seen before your eyes go through life with no intent but to frolic, to make merry and to laugh. It is said that the young who fall and are seduced into their camp return not unto their own but stay with the creatures who think not and cannot reason to know what is good and what is evil. It is said that if in your ramblings you should hear this laughter in the wood behind a tree, tarry not, but turn and go the other way. It is said that this is difficult to do when one is young."

> The laughter is sweet, it tickles the heart.
> The women are comely to look at and fun to be near.
> It is said that one must be strong to turn and go the other way.
> The laughter is sweet, we did hear it this night, you and I.
> It is also bitter, because he will die with it on his lips
> Should he succumb and turn not the other way.

George Clutesi

THE POTLATCH SONG OF QWAXILA

A Potlatch is held as part of any important ceremony — the naming of a child, the marriage of a daughter, the death of a chief. It is a method of establishing prestige and power as well as credit.

The host, with the help of his relatives, throws a huge party at which everyone gets expensive gifts and is feasted and entertained in the most lavish manner the host can manage.

Only a chief can hold a potlatch and only a great chief can hold a great potlatch. The guests must repay the host with interest or be shamed by the unpaid debt.

Qwaxila was a great Kwakiutl chief.

THE POTLATCH SONG OF QWAXILA

I am the only great tree,
I the chief!
I am the only great tree,
I the chief!
You are here right under me,
Tribes!
You are my younger brothers under me,
Tribes!
You sit in the middle in the rear of the house,
Tribes!
You surround me like a fence,
Tribes!
I am the first to give you property,
Tribes!
I am your Eagle,
Tribes!
Ya, ye, ā, ā, ye ya!

I wish you would bring your counter of property.
Tribes!

A fair breeze.

That he may in vain try to count what is going to be given away
By the great copper maker,
The chief,
Ya, ye, ā, ā!

Go on!
Raise the unattainable potlatch pole,
For this is the only thick tree
The only thick root
Of the tribes.
Ya, ye, ā, ā!

Now our chief will become angry in the house,
He will perform the dance of anger.
Our chief will perform the dance of fury.
I shall suffer from
The short life maker of our chief
Ya, ye, ā, ā!

I only laugh at him
I sneer at him
Who empties (the boxes) in his house
His potlatch-house
And the inviting-house that is the cause of hunger
All the house dishes are in the greatest house
Of our chief
Ya, ye, ā, ā!

MY PEOPLE THE HAIDA

La-ging-quo-na, Roar of the Breakers, also known as the Reverend Peter Kelly, was both United Church minister and Haida hereditary chief. He fought unrelentingly for the rights of Indian people without losing the respect of his white friends. He was a born teacher and loved nothing better than to share his rich and varied life with those who had never experienced two different worlds. In a nation-wide radio broadcast Mr. Kelly gave the following description of the Haida world he knew as a boy.

The homes of my people on the Queen Charlotte Islands were made entirely of red cedar. Each house was about fifty feet square, with side walls fourteen feet high and a gabled roof twenty feet. The frame and ridge pole were logs three feet in diameter, and the walls were planks four feet wide and four inches thick. Before the white man came, these planks were split from red cedar logs with bone wedges and stone mallets. The cedar grew from sixty to one hundred feet high below the branches and, therefore, it was easy to split as it was free from knots. In front of the house stood a fifty-foot totem pole carved from top to base. In the earlier times the door itself was merely an opening four feet high at the base of the pole. There were no partitions inside, just one large room with a fireplace in the middle, and two or three tiers of heavy planks around the walls, on which the inmates worked and slept. A gap in the roof served as a chimney; it could be opened or closed with a trap door.

Picture now, if you will, this massive house standing in a row with twenty or thirty similar houses along a gravel beach, and with the totem poles, both house-pole and mortuary, standing in a row in front of these houses, presenting quite an imposing picture as one approached the village from the sea. On nearer approach you would see many canoes on the beach, and people engaged in different activities. The men would be making canoes, paddles, long spears, bows and arrows, and fishing paraphernalia for halibut and other kinds of fishing. In the spring large racks of sliced halibut would be seen drying in the sun.

Haida village.

Fish-eggs, as herring spawn were called, would be seen drying in abundance. There would be seaweed also and many other varieties of foodstuff. In the autumn dog salmon, cohoes, and humpback choked the streams. These were either speared or trapped in great quantities and dried for food. Everybody worked, young and old alike. In the summer and early autumn the women gathered wild berries. The huckleberry, the salal berry, the high bush cranberry, other kinds of berries, and crabapples were gathered in and cured to be put away in boxes. Various kinds of wild roots were gathered in for food purposes. The potato was unknown in our Pacific coast until 1791 when it was introduced by a white fur-trader. The white men, of course, first got potatoes from the South American Indians. Ducks and geese were very plentiful, and seal and sea-lion, as well as porpoises, could be killed nearly all the year round and dried for food. Athough there were no game animals to be got on the Queen Charlotte Islands, there was no shortage of food. Of course the sea took its toll of those who braved it. The words of the poet, "Men must work, and women must weep," apply to all mankind, but particularly to those who follow the sea.

Houses, such as I have just described, are no longer to be seen; they were abandoned over fifty years ago. I was born in one, but lived and was raised in a modern house; for all the Haidas now live in modern houses. The sudden change from the large, well-ventilated community house to the air-tight modern house has been, in my opinion, injurious to the health of my people.

Many white people believe that we worshipped the totem poles that stood in front of our houses; that they were like the graven images before which the old heathens used to bow down. But our totem poles were not idols. We never prayed to them or reverenced them in any way. They resembled rather the coat of arms of European lords and knights. We had our nobles just as Europeans had, and it was only a nobleman who might erect a totem pole on the occasion of his accession to the family title. The pole was a tribute to his ancestors; and the birds and animals, real or imaginary, that were carved on its face were creatures that tradition said had played a part in the adventures of these ancestors.

The erection of a pole was no light matter. First of all the nobleman hired a trained sculptor to cut down a suitable cedar tree in the forest and to work on it, day after day, in absolute privacy. No one might see his carvings, not even the nobleman who had ordered them, until the work was completed. Then when the sculptor had finished his task, the tribesmen dragged the pole to the village, messengers sped up and down the coast in swift canoes to invite distinguished guests, and the family of the nobleman made its final preparations for the feasting and entertainment of perhaps one thousand people during one and perhaps even two weeks. In the early days they had to spend two or three years in gathering the necessary presents and food.

Peter R. Kelly

SONGS OF THE NOOTKA

The Nootka are famous for their songs among both Indian and non-Indian people. In 1788 a European called Meares was so impressed by Nootka singers that he wrote:

> *"We listened to their songs with an equal degree of surprise and pleasure. It was indeed impossible for any ear susceptible of delight from musical sounds . . . to remain unmoved by this . . . concert."*

Their songs are infinite in variety and are poetic as well as melodic. These three were collected by Frances Densmore.

Nootka method of spearing fish.

A PLEA FOR FAIR WEATHER

You, whose day it is, make it beautiful.
Get out your rainbow colours,
So it will be beautiful.

COMPLAINT AGAINST THE FOG

Don't you ever,
You up in the sky,
Don't you ever get tired
Of having the clouds between you and us?

LOST LOVE

No matter how hard I try
to forget you,
you always
come back to my mind,
and when you hear me singing
you may know
I am weeping for you.

OUR SAD WINTER HAS PASSED

Chief Dan George is a hereditary chief of the Coast Salish tribe of North Vancouver. He is also an actor and has played roles for C.B.C. television and the National Film Board. He has completed a movie with the Walt Disney Company in Hollywood. His faith in the future of his people is expressed in this soliloquy which he gave in the Playhouse Theatre, Vancouver, in the spring of 1968.

You call me Chief and you do well for so I am. The blood of chieftains flows in my veins. I am a chief but you may ask where are my warriors, their feathered heads, their painted faces.

I am a chief but my quiver has no arrows and my bow is slack. My warriors have been lost among the white man's cities, they have melted away into the crowds as once they did into the forests, but this time they will not return. Yes, my quiver is empty and my bow is slack.

Yes, I could make new arrows and I could tighten my bow but what little use it would be for my arrow would not carry very far as once it did. The bow has been reduced to a plaything. What was once a man's weapon is now a children's toy.

I am a chief but my power to make war is gone and the only weapon left me is my speech. It is only with tongue and speech that I can fight my people's war.

Today my people are tempted to look into the past and say "Behold our noble forebears".

Perhaps it is pleasant to look to the ages gone by and speak of the virility that once was ours. But the red man can never return to his campfire and forest. His campfire no longer exists outside of his own dreams.

He will wear out many moccasins walking, searching, searching and he will never return from the journey when that he seeks is no longer there.

It was during the first hundred years of Canada's nationhood that we met defeat. Broken by wars and disease we huddled on our reserves and nursed our wounds.

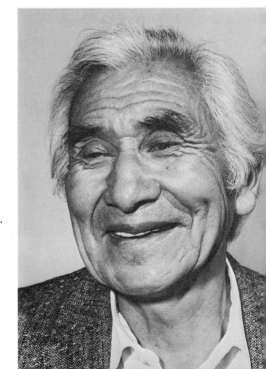

Chief Dan George.

But our greatest wound was not of the flesh but in our spirit and in our souls. We were demoralized, confused and frightened. We were left without weapons to defend ourselves, medicine to heal us, and leaders to guide us.

How easily despair comes when hope dies. How easily ambitions alter when goals slip from one's reach like the end of the rainbow.

How easily one says Oh, hell, what's the use, and then he dies within himself. How easily drink, drug, and vice come when pride and personal worth are gone.

But after the winter cold and icy winds life again flows up from the bosom of mother earth and mother earth throws off her dead stalks and the withered ends for they are useless and in their place new and strong saplings arise.

Already signs of new life are rising among my people after our sad winter has passed. We have discarded our broken arrows and our empty quivers for we know what served us in the past can never serve us again.

In unprecedented numbers our young men and women are entering fields of education. There is a longing in the heart of my people to reach out and grasp that which is needed for our survival.

There is a longing among the young of my nation to secure for themselves and their people the skills that will provide them with a sense of purpose and worth. They will be our new warriors, their training will be much longer and more demanding than it was in the olden days. Long years of study will demand determination. Separation from home and family will demand endurance.

But they will emerge with their hand held forward not to receive welfare but to grasp a place in society that is rightly ours.

The signs of this rebirth are all around us. There are more and more of our young men and women graduating from high school and their numbers will grow and grow within the next hundred years until the red man of Canada will once again stand firm and secure on his own two feet.

Dan George

DAMIAN

Damian, grandson of the famous Salish chief Dan George, caught pneumonia and had to go to the hospital. For his mother, Amy Marie George, this separation was very painful and she wrote this lovely poem about him.

DAMIAN

Damian darling,
son of mine
joy and happiness of life,
light of my cloudy days
and nights.
Little toddler so sweet, small
yet so strong
with such power
how can I endure this pain of partedness
with the squeals of your delight
still echoing through these still
silent walls
tearing
burning
hurting
this mother's heart of mine.
Oh, baby son of mine
how did I spend the hours
before you came to me
and where was I
when I was not with you.
Now, as I sit
this ache within my breast
waiting

hoping for that peaceful moment when,
once more
I hold your baby's flesh
to me again
and flow this love
welded up inside of me
into your own heart.

Amy Marie George

THE TOTEM POLE OF SAKAU'WAN

*It is rivalry which has often caused man to break records and pro-
duce great works of art. Today, the rivalry between the United States
and Russia has led men to the moon. One hundred years ago, on the
Nass River, rivalry led Tsimshian men to the production of elaborately
carved totem poles.*

*In 1927, Chief Mountain told this story of how the world's tallest
totem came into existence to Mr. Marius Barbeau. After his death in
1928 the pole was taken to the Royal Ontario Museum in Toronto
where all eighty-one magnificent feet of it are still on view.*

The Killer-Whale chief, Sispagut, who headed the faction of the earlier occupants on the river, announced his determination to put up the tallest pole ever seen in the country. Its name was to be Fin-of-the-Killer-Whale. However, instead of selecting for its carver Hladerh whose right it was to do the work, he chose Oyai of the canyon. Hladerh naturally felt slighted and confided his grudge to Sakau'wan, chief of the Eagles, and his friend. From then on the Eagles and the Wolves of their own day were to be closely allied, as the ancestors of both had moved in from Alaska and at one time had been allies.

Sispagut selected the largest red cedar he could find on Observatory Inlet, and had it towed down to the Nass. There his carver began to work. But Hladerh, now sure of the support of the Eagle clan, summoned Sispagut to shorten his "walking stick" by many arms' length; it was far too long! Sispagut ignored the protest. Insistent, Hladerh resorted to threats. Because of this, the tree remained under cover on the shore for a long time. But eventually Sispagut resolved to go ahead in the face of difficulties, and had Oyai resume his carving. When the pole was ready, he sat in his dug-out with his two wives and while he sang one of his dirges, he let it drift down the river in front of the village of Angyadae. The dirge meant that all the villages were invited to the feast for the erection of the pole. As he passed in front of Hladerh's house, the door opened, and a gun was fired at him. He fell down, wounded in the arm. The pole remained on the ground for another year. But the next spring a new date was announced for its erection. One night he [Sispagut] was betrayed by one of his nephews and shot dead. His heirs, however, refused to be intimidated, and later defiantly put up the totem pole of the Fin-of-the-Killer-Whale in memory of their uncle Sispagut. For a time it had won for them the supremacy of their clan on the river. The Eagles and the Wolves were newcomers, and had been thrown back in their own tracks.

This only sharpened the conflict between the two factions. Sakau'-wan (Sharp-Teeth) and Hlaherh searched for the largest cedar on Portland Canal, and found a perfect giant in Granby Bay, niney miles away. They had it cut down and towed to Gitiks. Oyai, the leading carver, once more was engaged to do the carving, along with four helpers. Although they toiled at it from dawn to sunset during the whole winter, it seemed as though their work would not be ready by the date fixed for its erection, after the end of the candle-fish season (in the spring). Invitations had been broadcast to the chiefs of neighbouring nations — the Tsimshians of the Skeena, the Haida of Queen Charlotte Islands, and the Tlingits of Tongas and Cape Fox, in Alaska. Everybody was keenly anticipating the contest between the Eagles and the Wolves on one side, and the Killer-Whales on the other. The guests were already beginning to land, but the carving of thirteen figures was not quite finished. Oyai had called in more helpers while the elders fretted, fearful of ridicule, and the pole was declared ready at the last possible moment.

Large crowds lent a hand and pulled at the stout cedarbark ropes or the nettle ropes made of old candle-fish nets, which were tied at three places on the long shaft. A trench leading to the hole was dug, into which the butt of the pole sank slowly. Thick planks held in place the crumbling earth around the pit; supporting posts were planted here and there; and trestles, pushed under the rising shaft, made progress secure at every inch gained, while a huge crowd pulled the ropes. Women sang haul-away songs and beat skin drums, to urge the workers at the ropes. Higher and higher went the pole, the face of its carvings mounting toward the sky. Whenever any dirt fell into the pit, a chief of high standing, who was called forth, stepped down, cleaned it out with his hands, and was liberally compensated for his service.

For two days the crowds pulled at the fibre ropes. Then a half-breed trader, Matheson, arrived at Gitiks in his sloop and saluted them with a gunshot. He would assist them with his tackle — ropes and other machinery recently acquired from white seamen. It was the first time that ropes of this kind, which seemed much stronger than their own, were used in this country. Haul-away songs instilled fresh vigour into the workers, the drums beat still louder, and soon the pole was nearly erect. But it was only at the close of the third day that the triumphant Eagle and Thunderbird reached their lofty destination in the sky.

Sharp-Teeth and his nephew, Mountain, came forward in full regalia, at the height of their glory. This was the greatest moment of their lives. They sang the sacred song of their ancestors: "The Golden

Eagle of the mountains will spread his wings, as he sits above the chiefs on the hilltops."

The Killer-Whales, the earliest Nass River occupants, now thrown back, had to accept their final defeat. They sat low and praised the Eagles with the rest, and cursed them under their breath. The Killer-Whales that day moved back from the front rank. The Eagles and the Wolves stood close to shore, facing the sea, and spoke for all others behind them on the Nass, under the shadow of the huge Eagle totem at the village of Gitiks.

To humble his rivals further, the Eagle chief, Sharp-Teeth, stood that night in front of his new pole and, close to a blazing fire, related at full length the story of his tribal migrations from the Far North to the blessed land of Leesems.

Thus came into existence the pole of Sakau'wan, the tallest and one of the finest monuments of its kind on the north Pacific coast. And the Eagle's Nest pole, the next best, soon followed in the wake, to make doubly secure the predominance of the Eagle-Wolf invaders over the older, native clan of the Killer-Whales.

As told to Marius Barbeau

Chapter II

Mountain People

The Mountain people live by the canyons of the racing salmon-spawning rivers — on the banks of lakes so deep no one knows that prehistoric monsters do not live there — and on the forest slopes of the spectacular British Columbia Mountains. The tribes are known as Lillooet, Thompson, Okanagan, Lake, Shuswap, Carrier, Chilcotin, and Kootenay.

This is the land of the ancient ones, and the valleys have sheltered them for thousands of years back to an ice-bound past. The record of the past is told by the "Indian paintings" found on cliffs and boulders throughout central British Columbia but the key to these stories is lost. Today we can only marvel and wonder.

Divided and separated by a geography that would isolate less adventurous people these people traded property, slaves, and ideas from the Pacific Ocean to the Prairies and adopted those ways of other peoples which suited them best.

The Mountain people have changed their ways many times over the centuries and have no fear of changes now. From the past they bring a strong belief in the equality of man, in peaceful coexistence and a devotion to individual freedom and responsibility. They farm. They ranch. They fish. They run businesses. They write poetry, and they run for Parliament. They are Canadians.

COYOTE AND THE MONSTER OF THE COLUMBIA

In the old "before people days" when animals were giants, Coyote was the most powerful of all. Being powerful did not mean that he was always wise or good. On the contrary he was often vain, boastful, and greedy. Occasionally he did help the lesser animal people and, good or bad, he was responsible for making the world the way we people found it.

One time on his travels, Coyote learned that a monster was killing the animal people as they travelled up and down Big River in their canoes. So many had been killed that some of the animal people were afraid to go down to the water, even to catch salmon.

"I will help you," promised Coyote. "I will stop this monster from killing people."

But what could he do? He had no idea. So he asked his three sisters who lived in his stomach in the form of huckleberries. They were very wise. They knew everything. They would tell him what to do.

At first his sisters refused to tell Coyote what to do.

"If we tell you," they said, "you will say that that was your plan all the time."

"If you do not tell me," said Coyote sternly, "I will send rain and hail down upon you."

Of course the berries did not like rain and hail.

"Do not send rain," they begged. "Do not send rain or hail. We will tell you what to do. Take with you plenty of dry wood and plenty of pitch, so that you can make a fire. And take also five sharp knives. It is Nashlah at Wishram that is killing all the people. He is swallowing the people as they pass in their canoes. You must let him swallow you."

"Yes, my sisters, that is what I thought," replied Coyote. "That was my plan all the time."

Coyote followed his sisters' advice. He gathered together some dry wood and pitch, sharpened his five knives, and went to the deep pool where Nashlah lived. The monster saw Coyote but did not swallow him, for he knew that Coyote was a great chief.

Coyote and the Monster of the Columbia by Saul Terry

Coyote knew that he could make Nashlah angry by teasing him. So he called out all kinds of mean names. At last the monster was so angry that he took a big breath and sucked Coyote in with his breath. Just before entering his mouth, Coyote grabbed a big armful of sagebrush and took it in also.

Inside the monster, Coyote found many animal people. All were cold and hungry. Some were almost dead from hunger, and some were almost dead from cold.

"I will build a fire in here for you," said Coyote. "And I will cook some food for you. While you get warm and while you eat, I will kill Nashlah. I have come to help you, my people. You will join your friends soon."

With the sagebrush and the pitch, Coyote made a big fire under the heart of the monster. The shivering people gathered around it to get warm. Then with one of his sharp knives Coyote cut pieces from the monster's heart and roasted them.

While the people ate, Coyote began to cut the cord that fastened the monster's heart to his body. He broke the first knife, but he kept cutting. He broke the second knife, but he kept cutting. He broke his third and his fourth knives. With his fifth knife he cut the last thread, and the monster's heart fell into the fire.

Just as the monster died, he gave one big cough and coughed all the animal people out on the land.

"I told you I would save you," said Coyote, as the animal people gathered around him on the shore of the river. "You will live a long time, and I will give you names."

Coyote went among them and gave each creature a name.

"*You* will be Eagle, the best and the bravest bird. *You* will be Bear, the strongest animal. *You* will be Owl, the big medicine man, with special powers. *You* will be Sturgeon, the largest fish in the rivers. *You* will be Salmon, the best of all fish for eating."

In the same way Coyote named Beaver, Cougar, Deer, Woodpecker, Blue Jay, and all the other animals and birds. Then he named himself. "I am Coyote," he told them. "I am the wisest and smartest of all the animals."

Then he turned to the monster and gave him a new law. "You can no longer kill people as you have been doing. A new race of people are coming, and they will pass up and down the river. You must not kill all of them. You may kill one now and then. You may shake the canoes if they pass over you. For this reason most of the canoes will go round your pool and not pass over where you live. You will kill very few of the new people. This is to be the law always. You are no longer the big man you used to be."

The law that Coyote made still stands. The monster does not swallow people as he did before Coyote took away his big power. Sometimes he draws a canoe under and swallows the people in it. But not often. Usually the Indians take their canoes out of the water and carry them round the place where the monster lives. They do not pass over his house. He still lives deep under the water, but he is no longer powerful.

* * *

The first steamboat the white people brought up the river was stopped by Nashlah. The Indians told the white men to throw food into the river and then they could go. They did so. They threw overboard sugar, flour, rice, and other things. Then Nashlah let the boat loose.

Collected by Ella Elizabeth Clark

FACES

Saul Terry, the young Lilooet sculptor from Bridge River, is also a poet. After graduating from the Vancouver School of Art in 1967, he began making his living as a sculptor, artist, and poet. In 1968, he took on the directorship of an all-Indian art school in Victoria where the curriculum is dictated by the talents and interests of the students.

FACES

When
   on the
      streets
       I
   pass
  a
  dark
face,
I wonder what he thinks of
          faces
          that
          pass
          him
           by,
         mostly
         pale?
         Does
       he
     detest
    them
   all,
   not
   knowing
   whether
  they
  be
good in
heart. Perhaps he's
     of
    open
    mind
    and
    takes
    them
    one
    for
    one to judge
         when
         they
         utter
        thoughts
           to
        him;
      and
    if
   this
   he
   does
no greater gift can he
attain for he is then a
           man.

Saul Terry

Indian picture-writing on walls at Radium Hot Springs, B.C.

TETLANEETSA

Without a vision a man is nothing; without a supernatural power he is defenceless against all enemies. Through fasting, praying, and solitary living, young men won for themselves a supernatural helper whose power became their power.

Each man's vision was personal, sacred, and secret. The guardian spirit often requested that certain songs and religious ceremonies be performed. Right action increased power and sometimes enabled a person to become a great chief (shaman). Tetlaneetsa, the Thompson chief, was one of the lucky men who obtained two powerful snams.

At fifteen years of age I stayed many moons in the mountains, undergoing my training, all alone, all alone.

I slept in the grass, one summer night, in an open space, near a patch of fireweeds. The wind rose at dawn and I heard a voice, a sweet voice, floating above, floating back and forth with the white cotton tufts from the fireweeds.

"Dear son, listen to me, listen to my song!"

Opening my eyes, I looked around, but could see no one. Only the wind went on, singing its song, a dream song — a *sekwalah*.

Slowly I woke up and again I heard the voice of the wind; it grew louder and clearer to my ears. It was a voice of many tones, as if people afar had been singing together, singing very softly at dawn, in a dream.

Now I understood the words of my old grandfather:

"When you wake up in the mountains at daybreak, you shall hear the voice of nature. Listen to it, son, for it holds treasures for you."

I listened to the voice of the wind, the voice from the valleys below growing louder with the light of dawn. Its song brushed the grass, the fireweeds, the bushes; it swept the treetops.

The rivers, the canyons, the mountain gorges, the forests, the wild fruit patches at timber line, and the peaks glittering with snow, they were all singing in the wind.

And I joined in the song of dawn, the song that was sweet, dream-like, endless — and mighty.

The wind of dawn woke me, the wind blowing up the mountain slopes. I learned their song and began to hum it to myself. Then I picked up my hat and used it as a drum. It was impossible to sit still, for the song floated on the air, and everyone must dance when the grass, the brush, and the treetops dance in the wind.

What did I see gliding out of the gates of sunrise? Two young women — the Twin Sisters. They were not walking; their feet only swept the weeds as they drifted in the wind. They sang the song of Nature as they slowly approached, picking flowers, blades of grass, and leaves wet with dew. Singing all the while until they were quite near.

Now they stood close to me like a dream of night, yet they were a vision of daylight. The elder sister had vermilion stars painted on her cheeks and the younger red moons on her breasts. The stars and the moons were like flowers raised above the surface, yet they were the scars of healed wounds.

Never had I seen the like of the Twin Sisters, the sisters of dawn. I fell prostrate to the ground before them. They both stooped over me and brushed my head and my shoulders with their soft leaflike hands.

Under their breath as they still sang, I passed from childhood to the rising power of a man.

The Twin Sister said to me: "Look at us, Brother, and see these healed wounds in our flesh."

"Yes, Sisters, I see them."

"The wounds came to us when we were shot, shot at by hunters. But we did not die, we could not die, because of our song, the Song of the Wind at daybreak.

"Sing our song, Brother, and it shall make you strong, strong as the weeds, strong as the trees. When a bullet pierces your flesh, sing it and paint vermilion on the wound as we have done, and like us you shall be well again."

And with them I sang the song of the Twin Sisters, in the rising sunlight.

When I awoke and looked up, the Twin Sisters of dawn had turned back with the morning wind; they were drifting away like two white clouds above the prairie stretching upwards toward the sunrise.

"Brother," they said, turning to me, "the hunters who shot us cannot do any harm, for we have sung the song of the wind, the song of all nature."

Before they had vanished into the forest they threw their song into the beak of Salalaw, the diver. And Salalaw repeated it while they cast off their shining garments and changed into bears, two female black bears, henceforth my own *snams* — my guardian spirits.

Eight years then followed like a gap in my life, eight full years without a glimpse of my snams. The snams are forgetting us nowadays; they are leaving the country. I was working on a Government trail, working with pick and shovel. As I slept there at night, I had a dream. The Twin Sisters appeared to me, singing the song of Nature, and they asked:

"Do you recognize it?"

I had recognized it, but there was no spirit left in me; I could not reply.

"Do you still remember us, the Twin Sisters?" they wondered. And I could only nod Yes.

I began to sing my dream song, sing it aloud in my sleep. I was still singing it when I awoke. And the Twin Sisters seemed to be standing near me, singing likewise. A white man, one of the white labourers in the next tent, opened his tent flap and wanted to stop me, asking me whether I was insane.

"No, I am not," I replied. "I had a dream. If I don't sing now, tomorrow I shall die."

The white men laughed — they did not believe in dreams, in guardian spirits. In spite of this, I kept on singing with all my power, singing through the night until dawn, singing the song of the Twin Bears that made me share in the strength of all the snams on earth, in the water, and in the air.

In the morning I went out as usual with my pick and shovel. With three Indians and many other workmen I walked past Siwash Creek to a deep ravine three miles away where stood two tall trees on the edge of the cliff. Unknown to us, a large tree trunk was lying there on its side above our heads as we passed below.

"Look out!" shouted an Indian.

The tree trunk was sliding down the hillside. I was caught by the tree and carried like a bullet a hundred feet below, between the trunk and another large log resting on the bottom near the water's edge.

The people cried out, "He is dead!"

I was not dead, only half asleep and half awake, as in a dream. My song was still inside me singing, the song of life. I could hardly breathe, I was choking.

The men chopped the tree trunk and drew me out of a hollow the size of my body between two large limbs. I was not dead, only fainting.

"Are you still alive?" they asked me.

I nodded; I was too feeble to speak. But my song was still singing in me; it kept on singing and giving me strength. Soon I could sit up, stand up. For many days I stayed in camp, very weak, but I never ceased to sing the Twin Bear song in my heart, the song that had saved my life.

From the personal reminiscences of Tetlaneetsa

Hector McIntyre, of the Skuppah Band near Lytton, B.C., is an experienced bulldozer operator.

THE LAST CRACKLE

In the February 1968 issue of the Vancouver Indian Centre magazine, The Telling Stone, *Gordon Williams had this to say:*

"I come from Vernon, British Columbia. My father was an Okanagan and my mother Shuswap so that makes me an amalgamation of two tribes. I've been attempting to write poetry for the last two years. I think I may one day be able to."

THE LAST CRACKLE

She sat there by the west window
Unmindful of the mosquitoes who'd always
Manage to squeeze thru the screen mesh
Insect barrier. Now it was sunset
Again, so many days of waiting.

A long time ago there were hardly
Any bearded men, now the forests are full!
They've flung bridges across all our rivers
And even our lakes. The sky is filled with metal
Birds that make noise loud as thunder.

All our men are dead and our young ones
Have no ambition. They took it all away,
Those bearded men, with their strange ways,
"Kneel with us" they said, "and pray!"
Then they took our land and children.

Now they've taken their beards off and shorn their
Hair, and they smile quick as a rattler's strike;
Before you open your door, a face of stone,
Then before your door is fully open, a smile
Trying to sell an old woman beauty cosmetics.

Her eyes were closed, she seemed to be asleep
Her drifting took her back a hundred years or more to
When she was just a little girl throwing pebbles making ripples
On the water's picture of white poplar trees.
Her days of waiting were ended, her chair
Rocking her away, and the last rays washing her face,
While the chair gave away the last crackle.

Gordon Williams

THOUGHTS ON SILENCE

Mary Jane Sterling is a member of the Thompson River (Nteakya-pamuk) Indian Band. She wrote the following comment on school life when she was many miles away from her home in central British Columbia attending school on Vancouver Island.

THOUGHTS ON SILENCE

What am I doing here
Among these strange people
Sitting in these funny desks
Staring at this paper?
Oh yes, I am in school.
These people are my classmates.
Though they chatter all the time
They are silent now.
Now I can think.
I see a bird flying high in the air.
Maybe it is flying south.
My heart leaps with the bird
Taking a message to my mother.
My mind is heavy, thinking something sad has
Happened at home.
But the birds are singing
Everything is all right.
The breeze has whispered something in my ear.
I hope it whispers the same joyous words to my people.
I get lonely for my family and I especially miss my mother
But I shall see them all soon.

When we meet we won't even touch hands
But our hearts will leap with joy
And in our minds we will be glad.

Mary Jane Sterling

LOSS FOR PROGRESS

*Clarence Oppenheim, a member of the Coldwater Band, was study-
ing painting and sculpture at the Vancouver School of Art when he
wrote this poem about "progress".*

LOSS FOR PROGRESS

High in the mountains
Where sound is lost
And occasionally found
By a Blue Jay's cry
The murmuring tree tops
Seem to be saying,
   "I hear machines
   and noise approaching
   Which means we will soon die".
As time passed
Only the faint cry
Of the Blue Jay's
Discontent was heard.

Gradually the remains
On the barren ground
Were but little trees
Planted row on row
And to visualize all the
Magnificence of Nature's Past
Is possible only
For the unbiased sky.

Clarence Oppenheim

COMING OF AGE

When Saul Terry was a student at the Vancouver School of Art he wrote the following comment on adolescence.

COMING OF AGE

A little frog inhales
(A bull to be, I assume was he)
His first croak on hand,
Deflates with a squeak;
Red faced (if ever one can be)
He leaps into the creek
Embarrassed (if ever frogs can be).

Saul Terry

THE HONOURABLE MEMBER FOR
KAMLOOPS-CARIBOO

On June 25, 1968, Mr. Leonard S. Marchand accomplished the unbelievable. He ran against and triumphed over the Honourable E. Davie Fulton in the Federal constituency of Kamloops-Cariboo. In doing so he not only defeated one of Canada's foremost statesmen but became the first Canadian Indian to gain a seat in the Canadian House of Commons. Who is Len Marchand? How did he win a federal election?

Perhaps he can best tell his story himself.

I went to the reserve day school for grades one to eight and to Kamloops Indian Residential School for grade nine. I took my high school in Vernon and even though I was the first student from our reserve to go to Vernon High, I thought it was great. I did feel a little apprehensive and a little lost for a while but my parents had friends in town and so, I found friends in high school that I'd known for quite a while. In a couple of months I was right at home and made a lot of new friends.

I completed high school in the general program then found I didn't have the required courses to go on to university, so I decided to take an extra year and pick up the subjects I needed for university entrance. In October of that year, when the first report card came out, I had a D in one of the maths and a D in something else. I was leaning on my locker outside the classroom just after I got my card. I decided I was going to quit, just going to pack it up. This was just not for me. One of my friends, a teacher, said: "Why don't you give it another try and see if it works." So, I went back and on my next report card my lowest mark was a C. I kept going and by the end of the year, I was recommended in all of my subjects. That was a really critical time in my life.

There were other people whose advice helped me too. We had a Band Counsellor one time, James Bonneau, an uncle of mine. He used to say, "Do things yourself. Look after yourself. Don't depend on the government." His words impressed me. He'd talk about the Indian way of life, the way our ancestors lived, and the pride they had in being independent and would say, "We got along in this world as individuals before the white men came." He is a rancher, a successful rancher. He has 300-400 head of cattle and has always been a very independent man. To him nature is important and the independence of his own people is important. We never talk much about being Indians on my home reserve. We don't go around wearing a headdress or saying: "I Am An Indian." We are Indians, fine, so what! We are more concerned about making our way in life as human beings, as individuals.

I really didn't think I could win against Davie Fulton in the election. When the guys first asked me to come out, I told them that they were crazy. "Who me, run against Davie Fulton?" But they said, "No, really, we think you have a chance. You have an education. You have three years' experience in Ottawa as the Special Assistant to two Ministers of Indian Affairs, the Honourable J. R. Nicholson and the Honourable Arthur Laing. You have a B.Sc. degree in Agriculture from the University of British Columbia and an M.Sc. in Forestry from the University of Idaho. You also have made a reputation in Kamloops as a responsible individual."

I did a lot of work in the Mika Nika Club in Kamloops. At that time there were no Indians working in town. Some of them just needed a helping hand so we showed them the ropes, simple things like how to apply for a job, and in four years we placed 150-200 people in Kamloops alone.

I'll have to admit that I didn't know much about a campaign. I had never been actively involved in politics before, but then politics is just people isn't it. You elect a man, not a politician. The most important thing is the ability to communicate with people. I used coffee parties. I had 120 between May 15th and June 25th. I wanted to meet as many people as possible and talk with them. They wanted to size me up as an individual and I wanted them to have that chance rather than telling them what they had already read in the newspapers or heard on the radio or television. I think they appreciated the opportunity of talking with me and discussing problems rather than listening to me telling them what I thought was good for them.

It costs money to get elected and I don't know how other candidates handled their fund raising, but my campaign chairman was in charge of raising money for me. I didn't know where any of the money came from, but he went out and asked businesses and individuals to contribute. There are many people who believe in participating in the running of the country. So they contribute. Just like supporting a church — the same sort of philosophy. It was fantastic the response we got. We had people coming in off the street and kicking in fifty cents, twenty-five cents, two dollars, three dollars. I was told that we had donations up to one thousand dollars.

I don't know how I beat Mr. Fulton but there's a lot to the old saying that you've got to be the right man, at the right place, at the right time. I was encouraged all the way, but we were all sort of down in the mouth on voting day. In the first results that came in, I was behind, but after six or seven polls, I started to pull ahead. One of the fellows who was coming in to report the results was just about hitting the ceiling. He was getting happier and happier and happier. It was really great. It was just a fantastic experience. To know that so many people had confidence in me was a great feeling.

I am the first Indian to sit as a member in the House of Commons and I am conscious of my responsibilities. I have an obligation which I could not escape if I wished to, and that is my obligation to my fellow Indians. I am an Indian who is a member of Parliament. I am not just the Indian people's member; but I must speak on their behalf.

Being elected for Kamloops-Cariboo was a great honour. I received another honour almost as great just after Parliament opened. Prime Minister Trudeau asked me to second the Address in Reply to the Speech From The Throne.

* * *

In his speech on September 13, Mr. Marchand was able to outline his feelings as a member of Parliament. He spoke about his riding and Canada in general but he devoted a portion of the speech to the Indian people particularly.

* * *

MR. SPEAKER: The Honourable member from Kamloops-Cariboo.

MR. MARCHAND (Kamloops-Cariboo): Honourable members know that the situation of many Indian families is deplorable. We all know that in respect of income, standards of health, and living conditions many Indian people are below that standard of acceptability in this country. They are isolated from their fellow Canadians and they are shut off from many aspects of Canadian life. I do not think that racial discrimination is a factor. In view of the honour the people of Kamloops-Cariboo have paid me how could I feel otherwise? It is just a cruel historical fact of life beyond the control of the Indian people. The efforts to bring them into the world of today and to their rightful place in Canada must continue.

Indians are a proud race. We have much in our past of which we are proud. Our culture can make an even greater contribution to Canada than the very considerable one it has already made. There is much about Indian life that is good and there is much for Canadians to learn about it. We have been held back but we are on the move today.

It is important for the younger Indians who are in school and at university to know that, with reasonable hope, they can aspire to become whatever they wish to become and are capable of becoming.

Leonard S. Marchand, Member of
Parliament for Kamloops-Cariboo, B.C.

It is important for all Canada to know that this is not a land of bigotry and prejudice. It is important for all Canadians to keep it that way.

Although the Indian people once held all this land and now have but little of it, although the Indian once was the master of his environment and is no longer, it is less than helpful to repine for times when things were different. No one can turn back the clock. The useful, the important, and the right thing to do is to master the environment that is.

I am sure every member of the House agrees that Canadians today, English-speaking Canadians, French-speaking Canadians, Indian Canadians, every kind of Canadian — all of us are looking ahead with the confidence born of a certainty that our country is capable of doing what has to be done, of correcting the defects of today to make a world in which we can be even prouder of being what we all are, Canadians, living in a great and fine land, a land which has much to offer the world, a land which has some problems but none that cannot be solved.

Leonard S. Marchard M.P.

Chapter III

The Confederacy

What proud people those Blackfoot! Tall, handsome and confident, they once reigned over all the cattle country of Alberta, western Saskatchewan and northern Montana. The three tribes, the Sik'sika (Blackfoot), the Kainai (Blood) and the Pikû'ni (Peigan) together with the Sarcee people who affiliate themselves with the Confederacy, made up this mighty nation whose world was wide as well as rich.

In the days when the dog was the only means of conveyance, life was hard, but the capture of the first horse from a southern neighbour opened a new world of riches and adventure. Hunting, raiding, and visiting over vast areas became possible. The horse was "money" and Blackfoot men counted their wealth in horses. Even after the Treaty, in the poor days — the starvation and sickness days — they kept the horses.

But the horse, the provider of wealth and adventure, proved less and less valuable in the modern world, and during the nineteen thirties and forties, hundreds disappeared into meat processing plants and the bellies of mink. The people found a new wealth in cattle, thousands of head, and in new breeds of horses, the thoroughbred, the appaloosa, and the palomino.

Although Blackfoot people today may work in many of the modern occupations, it is on the cattle ranch and the rodeo circuit where life takes on the right kind of flavour, and those who visit western Canada in July or August will probably find the people at the Stampede.

RODEO! Each summer, near Calgary, Alberta, the Blood people hold a rodeo on their own reserve that brings western cowboys flocking from miles around to pit their skill against bucking broncs and wild steers.

Rufus Goodstriker, former Blood Chief and his son, Wilton, adjust saddles after a hard day's ride over the prairie.

THE RACE

There are hundreds of stories about Napi (Old Man) who made the world amid many blunders. This particular story was told by Peigan warriors to George Bird Grinnell (an American anthropologist) at the beginning of the nineteenth century.

Once Old Man was travelling around, when he heard some queer singing. He had never heard anything like this before and looked all around to see who it was. At last he saw it was the cottontail rabbits singing and making medicine. They had built a fire, and got a lot of hot ashes and they would lie down in these ashes and sing while one covered them up. They would stay there only a short time though, for the ashes were very hot.

"Little Brothers," said Old Man, "that is very wonderful how you lie in those hot ashes and coals without burning. I wish you would teach me how to do it."

"Come on, Old Man," said the rabbits, "we will show you how to do it. You must sing our song and only stay in the ashes a short time." So Old Man began to sing and he lay down, and they covered him with coals and ashes, and they did not burn him at all.

"That is very nice," he said. "You have powerful medicine. Now I want to know it all, so you lie down and let me cover you up."

So the rabbits all lay down in the ashes, and Old Man covered them up, and then he put the whole fire over them. One old rabbit got out and Old Man was about to put her back when she said, "Pity me, my children are about to be born."

"All right," replied Old Man, "I will let you go, so there will be some more rabbits; but I will roast these nicely and have a feast." And he put more wood on the fire. When the rabbits were cooked, he cut some red willow brush and laid them on it to cool. The grease soaked into these branches, so even today if you hold red willow over a fire, you will see the grease on the bark. You can see, too, that ever since the rabbits have a burnt place on their backs where the one that got away was singed.

Old Man sat down, and was waiting for the rabbits to cool a little when a coyote came along, limping very badly.

"Pity me, Old Man" he said, "you have lots of cooked rabbits; give me one of them."

"Go away," exclaimed Old Man. "If you are too lazy to catch your food, I will not help you."

"My leg is broken," replied the coyote. "I can't catch anything and I am starving. Just give me half a rabbit."

"I don't care if you die," replied Old Man. "I worked hard to cook all these rabbits and I will not give any away. But I will tell you what we will do. We will run a race to that butte, way out there, and if you can beat me you can have a rabbit."

"All right," said the coyote. So they started. Old Man ran very fast, and the coyote limped along behind, but close to him, until they got near to the butte. Then the coyote turned round and ran back very fast for he was not lame at all. It took Old Man a long time to go back, and just before he got to the fire, the coyote swallowed the last rabbit and trotted off over the prairie.

George B. Grinnell

AKAINAH-MUKAH, THE SENATOR

When the boy who was later to become Senator James Gladstone was nine he received his personal name, Akainah-Mukah or "Many Guns". It was 1896. He grew up to become a successful rancher and farmer on the Blood Reserve before he became the first Indian appointed to the Senate. As a boy in the Anglican boarding school he was a great one for practical jokes. To revenge himself on a bully he made use of the fact that in those days Blackfoot people had a great fear of ghosts.

In the spring of 1894, I was taken to St. Paul's Anglican mission, which was located on Big Island on the Belly River, near the old whiskey fort of Slideout. This school had been built for the Blood Indians and, when I first saw it, it included a mission house, boys' home for seventy boys and staff, a church, barn, storehouse, and girls' dormitory. These were built in the form of a square. A hospital and rectory were added later on.

My brother, Steve, and I were admitted together. Steve was a timid person, so the other boys didn't bother him. But I was always getting into trouble and was the butt of their jokes. I remember one of their tricks was to throw me in among the burial places. One end of our island was heavily wooded and this was a favourite place for placing the dead. The Bloods used to wrap the dead in blankets and place them in the trees. When the supervisor took us for a walk, the boys would grab me by the hands and feet and throw me into these bushes. At first I was scared, but after a while I found that nothing happened to me, so I started poking around the bundles. That gave me an idea for getting even.

One of the ringleaders was Arthur White Buffalo Chief. So, on one of our daily walks, I picked up two skulls from the graves and smuggled them into the dormitory. When it was dark, I tied one of the skulls above Arthur's bed and another over Sydney Eagle Tail Feathers — another bully. Then I went back to bed and waited.

At night, the boys used to make cigarettes and pass them around from bed to bed. I heard the boy next to me rolling one. When he struck the sulphur match there was a moment's silence as he stared at the skull; then he shouted "Noo-aw". Arthur woke up and the first thing he saw in the flickering light of the match was the skull staring down at him. He didn't say a word, he just passed out. Right across from him George LaChappelle also fainted. But Sydney wasn't scared at all by the skull over his bed.

When the supervisor came in, I pulled the covers over my head and pretended I was asleep. He took the skulls away and no one ever found out who was responsible. But Arthur must have known, for from that time on he was a good friend of mine.

James Gladstone

The Remains by Ross E. Woods

EAGLE PLUME (PI'TA SAHWOPI)

In 1927 old friends of the Blood tribe met together at Waterton Lakes National Park in the Rocky Mountains of southern Alberta to talk about the old days. Among the group was Apikuni (James Willard Schultz), a white man who had married into the Peigan Tribe. He wrote down the stories that his friends told and published them in a book called The Sun God's Children. *This story is part of Eagle Plume's autobiography which he told the group around the campfire one night.*

Day came and revealed to us that which made our hearts glad: A little way farther up the valley, in a wide, grassed flat and near heavy timber bordering the river, was a circle of more than two hundred lodges. Lodges of new, white leather; whitely gleaming in the light of the rising sun. And tethered close to the lodges of their owners were many horses; the war horses, the fast, trained buffalo horses of which their owners were so proud. Other horses there were, many, many bands of them, grazing in the great bottom above, below, and out around the camp. Smoke was rising from the lodges; women were hurrying to the river for water; to the timber for fuel; men were going, some of them to battle, others were caring for their horses: they were rich, powerful people, our enemies, the Crows.

'Said Bear Bones: "It will be easy to take all of those far-out grazing horses that we can drive, but I don't want them. I want, I am going to have, some of those big, powerful, swift ones that are tied here and there in the camp."

'So said all the others of our party.

'In all that great camp, there was but one painted lodge; the Crows seemed to have few sacred-pipe men; anyhow there was but this one lodge that had sacred paintings upon it. A very large lodge it was, and well apart from the others, in the lower side of the circle. Two black and white spotted horses were tied in front of its doorway. Pointing to them, I said to my companions: "Those two there in front of the painted lodge, they are mine."

' "Yes. Yours, the two spotted ones," they answered.

'Just then a man came out of the painted lodge, untied the two horses, smoothed their manes and tails with a handful of brush, then led them to the river to drink. Presently he brought them back into the open, hobbled one and let it go, led the other back to his lodge, and saddled it. Many other men were saddling their swift animals; they were going out to run buffalo. I prayed to my medicine, to the Above Ones. "Pity me; help me. Let this be the last time that painted lodge man will ride that spotted fast one. Help me to take it and its spotted mate," I said.

'Sun was but a little way up in the blue when a hundred or more riders gathered at the lower side of the camp circle, and came down the valley, went down past us, talking, laughing, singing, happy all of them. And following them were their women, with travois horses and pack horses for bringing in the meat and hides of the killing that was to be made.

'Sun went to his island home. Night came, and we sneaked down into the valley and through the timber to the river, and drank plenty of water and ate of our dried meat.

'The night could not have been better for our raid; clouds hid Night-Light, above us, yet it was not too dark; we could see objects, make out what they were, at a distance of twenty or twenty-five steps. So it was that I surely but slowly approached the big painted lodge. To go to it, I had to pass between two lodges at the outer edge of the

Eagle Plume (Pi'ta Sahwapi),
Blood Warrior.

circle. When quite near them, I stopped, listened, heard in one of them the heavy breathing of a sleeper. I went on, and made out that a dark object that I was approaching was a horse; and then I saw that it was one of my black-and-white spotted buffalo runners. It did not flinch from me when I went right to it and stroked its shoulder. Its rope, I made out, was fastened to a peg of the lodge skin. I stood beside the horse, looking, listening. All was quiet. I believed that I knew where my other spotted one was tied. I went on past the door-way of the lodge and right to it, its rope end fastened also to a lodge peg. I noiselessly untied it, coiled it as I moved on to the horse, and then started leading him to the other one. But slowly: only a step or two at a time. When I had got right in front of the lodge, a sleeper within began dream-talking; not loud; a few words at a time. But I didn't like that; people who talk in their sleep wake up. This one might awake, hear the horses moving off, and come out. I was very uneasy; led the horse still more slowly; and at last came to the other one; and his rope I cut, at right length for leading him, and then I went on with the two, backing away from the painted lodge until I could no longer see it, then watching the two other lodges as I passed between them; on out, from the camp and at a faster pace to the point of timber. Several of my companions had already arrived there with takings of horses, and had gone again for more of them. Wolf Plume took charge of mine, and said: "Ha! The two spotted ones. You said, up there on the valley slope, that they were yours, and you spoke the truth; they are yours."

' "Yes. And now I go to the camp for more of them," I answered.

' "Wait. Hear me. Pity me, Sun-Power man," said he. "I have work-ed for you, carried your medicine things; do pity me; let me go at least once into this enemy camp and take horses, even one horse. I want to be a warrior. I want to be able to count at least one coup when, this summer, we build Sun's great lodge."

' "Yes. I do pity you," I answered. "When I come again, I will make some one take your place here, and you shall go to the camp with me."

'Again I led two horses to the meeting-place, and close following me came Bear Bones with three, making five that he had taken. I ask-ed him to remain there until Wolf Plume could make one entrance into the camp with me. He objected; said he had not come with me as a servant.

' "You were once as is this youth; anxious to count your first coup. Some one did for you as I now ask you to do for him," I answered.

' "True. Go, you two. I will watch our takings here," he said.

'I believed that my companions had none of them been in the upper part of the big camp, so I decided that we should try our luck up there. With Wolf Plume close at my side, and moving slowly, noiselessly, I passed between the two lodges just below the painted lodge, went by it, and two others, and was then in the grass and sagebrush bottom land that the circle of the lodges enclosed. It was maybe two hundred steps across. We were nearing the lodges at its upper side, were rounding an almost shoulder-high patch of sagebrush, when a man rose up close in front of us and spoke three or four words, no doubt asking who we were or where we were going. He never spoke again or even groaned; I struck the top of his head with the end of my rifle barrel, and with all my strength, and he dropped and Wolf Plume, who carried no gun, only bows and arrows in the case upon his back, gave a downward spring and stabbed him in his breast; and then whispered to me: "Here. Take my knife and scalp him."

' "I will take one side, you the other," I answered; and when we had done that, we felt about for any weapons that the dead one might have had, but could find none; not even a knife in his belt. He was not a night watcher for the camp, else he would have had a gun or a bow and arrows. He had recently come from his lodge for one purpose or another, had probably wakened his woman when leaving his couch, and she would become alarmed if he did not soon return to her, and would arouse the camp. I whispered to Wolf Plume that we must go on.

'We soon came to the lodges in the upper part of the circle and found that there were horses tied before all of them. We each took two, from lodges at the outer edge of the circle, and led them well out toward the edge of the bottom, and thence down to the meeting-place. Besides Bear Bones, four others were there with second and third takings, and close after us came in the rest, with one, and two, and even three more horses each.

54   I AM AN INDIAN

'Mounting each of us one of our takings, I led off, the others driving the loose horses after me; and we were not out of the bottom when we heard great shouting and crying back in that enemy camp. At that, we went on with all the speed that we could make with our little band of loose animals. But that, we felt, was fast enough, for we could frequently change on to fresh horses, and so outride any who might pursue us. Three times we so changed before we came to Elk River, and twice more after crossing it. And if any of the Crows did take our trail, we never saw them. We made the long way back to our people without trouble, and got great praise for our success. Yes, and one of the Sun lodge-builders of that summer was my woman.

'Kyi! I end my tale.'

James Willard Schultz

WE SIGN

Crowfoot was the most eloquent of the North Blackfoot and in matters of diplomacy the people gave him their trust. It was up to him to decide whether to sign the treaty with the white men. This responsibility weighed on him very heavily.

Mrs. Ethel Brant Monture describes Crowfoot's vital decision in her book Canadian Portraits.

The unrest in the councils spread through the camps and when the too-eager Oblates went to the old good chief, Natous, urging him to use his power to have Crowfoot make a good decision, Natous sent them away abruptly, saying, "When the time comes Crowfoot will speak." The Blackfoot would have to live under white laws. The priests said there would be no other way. Would these new laws, unknown to all of them, let them preserve the way of life that had built the people and made them respected on the plains? This was the worry that gnawed Crowfoot's mind. Father Lacombe busied himself by calling on all the chiefs of the Confederacy and some of them were offended by this. They were suspicious, for they had decoyed the buffalo into traps themselves and the eager priests now seemed to be trying to lure them into a snare.

On September 18, 1877 the "great men" came. The Honourable David Laird, Lieutenant-Governor of the North West Territories and Indian Superintendent, was one of them. He was a Canadian from Prince Edward Island. The other was Commissioner James Macleod of the North West Mounted Police. The Blackfoot had come to trust him when they saw that the Red Coats under his command gave him the same loyalty Crowfoot had earned from his people. In Scotland the forbears of Commissioner Macleod had known plenty of conflict, when border wars raged between England and Scotland and many of the settlers on the Red River in Manitoba were crofters or small farmers who had been dispossessed by tyrannous landlords in Scotland. Commissioner Macleod had sympathy for the Blackfoot, but he also had a stern duty before him. With the Honourable David Laird he was to lead the Blackfoot to "cede, release, surrender and yield up" to the government of Canada fifty thousand square miles of their prairie kingdom. For this land and in "extinguishment of all past claims" each man, woman and child was to be paid at once twelve dollars. Later there would be other benefits like cattle, medals, implements and a yearly payment forever of a few more dollars for each member of the tribe, with the chiefs in power getting the most.

The meeting place for the council was at Blackfoot Crossing, a favourite home camp of the people and a place of unusual beauty. On this September day the river glimmered in the sunshine and the cottonwoods and willows shone with golden leaves. The coulees were all aglow with the bronze and russet browns of the wild rose and buffalo berry bushes. The Confederacy made camp, a settlement of a thousand lodges. The Indians were in their finest clothing and each cooking fire sent a smoke signal high in the clear sky. A large tent had been erected to serve for a council chamber at one end of the encampment. The bell-shaped tents of the Mounted Police shone white at the other. The commissioners arrived in great style, escorted by officers of the police in their red coats and spiked helmets. After all were assembled in the large tent the council was opened with a fanfare from the police band.

Crowfoot would not accept any small gifts from the commissioners until the people had heard the terms of the treaty read. James Bird, the son of a Hudson's Bay Company employee who had taken an Indian wife, was the interpreter for them. They were very quiet and they asked time for conferring. They still had no real knowledge of the small acreage that ceding would confine them to, but the Confederacy trusted Crowfoot completely. If they had not, a rebellion might have flared up, and this could have had disastrous results. Crowfoot was under tremendous pressure.

He went to stay alone in his lodge and the commissioners waited impatiently. At last he gave the word that he would sign on the morn-

Crowfoot, head chief of the Blackfoot.

ing of the fifth day, September 22nd. Having made the decision, overwhelmed with worry and sorrow, he moved his lodge out of the camp circle to a lonely place.

When the morning of the fifth day came a cannon was fired from the hill as a signal that the council was to begin. The cannon boomed again as Crowfoot made his mark on the long parchment of the treaty, the bagpipes wailed gaily and the Union Jack was hoisted. The other chiefs of the Confederacy made their marks.

The Honourable Mr. Laird led off the speeches. He loved to make speeches. He spoke easily and cultivated an elegant manner. He also spoke intimately of the Great Spirit who had made them all brothers, the white man and the red, saying "We should take each other by the hand," and "the Queen is pleased that you have taken the Mounted Police by the hand and helped her by obeying her laws. If this is done they will always be your friends and on your side."

When Crowfoot made his speech he turned to Governor Laird, giving him a feather he had drawn from his eagle's wing fan, saying "Keep us like this feather forever." He expressed his worry and foreboding in this allegorical way. In time the young men, deprived of their life of hard riding and responsibility for providing the food for their people from the hunts, would be like the pliable feather he held. When that time came he hoped the commissioners would have patience. He felt that it would take a long, long time for his people to accept a changed way of life that would make them into another people.

By way of entertainment, after the signing was completed, the Confederacy staged a sham battle such as they enacted after a Sun Dance ceremony. This was really a mounted war dance. Hundreds of gaily dressed warriors encircled the whole encampment, performing riding feats and firing guns into the air. It was so realistic that the officials were alarmed and the warriors enjoyed their uneasiness. If the Red Coats could parade their strength, the Confederacy could put on a good show too.

Ethel Brant Monture

GONNA RIDE A BULL

Although the Sarcee live in Alberta and the Navajo in Arizona hundreds of miles to the south, they are relatives. Both are Athapaskans. In this poem Tommy Smith, the Navajo, talks about one interest the two people have in common — "cow punching".

GONNA RIDE A BULL

I'm gonna ride a bull.
    I'm a fool
A hop, a spin, a twist —
    Bull's are cool.

My mouth will get me killed
    I'm so brave.
While standing on the ground
    How I rave!

A boaster who can't ride —
    That's my speed.
My tongue should be cut out
    Oh, stampede!

Oh, well! I said I would
    Here goes, Bull
I'm on. Heigh ho! I'll never
    leather pull.

I need the worst you'll give
    Teach me now.
Defeat is sweet. Henceforth
    I'll ride a cow

And let
my tongue
come
wagging
along
behind.

Tommy Smith

Chapter IV

Sun's Land

In search of the buffalo and the enemy camp the Cree, Assiniboine, Sioux, and Gros Ventre people once travelled the entire stretch of rolling grassland now known as the prairie provinces. Though often at war with one another they had much in common; a love of the free, democratic life, a reverence for all of nature, and particularly the Sun — the Great Provider.

Battles there were, but by today's standards the people were peace loving. Skill in battle and in hunting was essential, but personal valour and generosity were valued above all else. Even the counting of coup (that badge of honour) emphasized personal bravery more than killing.

Life was difficult but the buffalo were plentiful. There was time to enjoy the world and the camps rang with laughter more often than tears. The people's love of fun was always present — even in serious legends about the beginning of time.

The suffering of the Sun's People since the white man came may have changed them in many ways but the man of courage with a big heart and a twinkling eye is still the hero. I hope that these stories from "The Land of the Sun" will help show the spirit of "the big people from the big land".

Canadian Geese by Francis Kagige

WESAKACHAK AND THE GEESE

In the beginning Wesakachak, the trickster, wandered through the country trying to fool everybody and everything. He was not always successful. Jackson Beardy, a young Cree artist and writer collected this story and it will be published together with other stories in book form with Mr. Beardy's own illustrations.

"I think I'll go for a walk," thought Wesakachak one day.

As he was walking by a lake, he spied a flock of geese feeding in the marshes.

"I'm hungry and I would love a goose for a meal. But I wonder how can I be able to get them over?" he thought to himself.

Finally, he produced a large leatherhide and went to the forest. Coming to a swamp, he picked up some moss and bundled it. Then he walked along the shoreline with his head down pretending he did not see the geese.

It did not take any time for the geese to notice him.

"Look at Wesakachak with the bundle on his back. Let's ask him what he's got in his bundle," one of them said.

"Wesakachak, what are you carrying?" they shouted to him.

Still Wesakachak did not seem to hear.

"Wesakachak, what are you carrying?" they shouted a little louder.

This time Wesakachak pretended to look around for the voices.

"What did you say?" Wesakachak shouted back.

"What are you carrying?"

"I am carrying my song-bag," Wesakachak said.

"Let's hear you sing then."

"Oh, I have to build a lodge in which to sing, my friends. Perhaps you would be kind enough to help me build it since you want to hear my songs that bad?"

After they had finished the lodge, Wesakachak started to sing. Making up songs as he went along. He gave instructions in song form as the geese danced them out. The loon danced in one spot by the doorway.

Soon Wesakachak began to run out of words. "Now we shall put our heads together," he sang.

And the geese danced with their heads together.

"I bring you the Shut-Eye Dance," he sang again. "Shut your eyes with your heads together and dance."

As the geese danced with their heads together, eyes closed, Wesakachak kept howling as he proceeded to lasso the flock of geese.

Just as he threw the leather rope, the loon by the door took a peek with one eye and howled at the top of his lungs, "Wesakachak is killing us all!" Some geese managed to escape, but as the loon was rushing out the doorway, Wesakachak gave him the biggest kick in his life on his rear end. To this day, the loon has a flat hip and cannot walk on land. The loon howls in the stillness of the wilderness, holding his rear end.

Jackson Beardy

PAYEPOT THE SIOUX-CREE CHIEF

The Plains Cree had many famous chiefs. Among the greatest was Payepot, the warrior, medicine man, and wise counsellor, whose reserve in Saskatchewan still bears his name and whose presence had an indelible effect upon all those who knew him. One of his greatest admirers was Herald In The Sky — Abel Watetch — who returned from school to the reserve where he began his second education by listening to Payepot's stories and teachings. He learned much before the great man died at the age of ninety-two. Part of Payepot's remarkable life is told for us here by Mr. Watetch.

'Way back in 1816 a party of Plains Crees were encamped near what is now the border between Canada and the United States. One very sultry day, when storm clouds had gathered low overhead, rumbling with the breath of the Thunder Bird, a son was born to a young Cree couple.

It was the custom of the Crees to name a child for whatever object or incident was first observed when the wail indicated a new life had begun. As this little Cree's cry began there was a great flash of lightning leaping across the blue sky. So the newcomer was named Kisikawawasan Awasis, or Flash-in-The-Sky-Boy.

He had a grandmother in the camp and this wise old woman felt that the child would some day be a great leader of the Crees, a medicine man, perhaps a chief. So she took over the care of the infant while the young parents resumed killing and preparing food for the band.

Not long after his birth, some of the hunters, far out on the prairie, came upon a lonely white man, who had been left behind by a party of explorers because he was ill. The hunters took the man back to camp and gave him shelter and food and tried to nurse him back to health. They did not know that the man had smallpox.

Smallpox was the terror of all Indians, since the first terrible epidemic had spread like fire among them a generation before this time, killing thousands of their kith and kin. The one instinct of the Indians was flight. So when they realized what had happened, they rode off in all directions, abandoning all those who were unable to follow them. Survival of the few depended on their ruthlessness, for there was nothing they could do to combat the horrible disease.

Presently there was no one left in the camp but the grandmother and her helpless charge. Neither of them was infected with smallpox, but the outlook was grim for there was no one to hunt for them and no other food within the reach of the old woman.

With the stoicism of the Indian she began setting up a shelter for herself and the child from the bits and pieces the others had left behind them and contrived a little tepee from oddments of buffalo hides.

She kept the child alive by going about gathering old buffalo bones and boiling them in a kind of bag made of buffalo hide hung on stakes, dropping hot stones into the water, to make soup.

Autumn was approaching and the old grandmother had no means of coping with winter weather that was not far off. But she went bravely on, buoyed up by her secret belief that this was a child destined for greatness.

Some dogs had also been abandoned and one day as she was sitting with the child on her knees, she noticed that the dogs were uneasy and restless and sometimes howled. She pricked up her ears, because it seemed to portend that someone or something was not far off.

It was some time before a party of Sioux [also a hunting party] came from the south, right to the campsite. She was terrified of the traditional enemy of her people and had hidden in her shelter. The Sioux, when they saw human bodies lying about, turned to ride away. But one of them saw a movement under the shelter and so they rode over to the pile of skins.

When they found the old lady with a fine boy in her arms, they took them both prisoners and rode off with them towards Dakota.

In the Sioux country the woman and the child were well cared for. The boy grew up speaking Sioux and was taught all the skills of a Sioux hunter and warrior.

When he was about fourteen years of age, a Cree war party surprised this band of Sioux and since war was a game and a skill, just as was buffalo hunting, they attacked the Sioux camp and put them to rout. Then the grandmother, seeing the attackers and hearing their familiar voices cried out that she was a Cree and pointed out Kisikawawasan Awasis, telling them who he was. She convinced them, and the victorious Crees rode away to the north carrying the boy and his grandmother with them, back to their favourite country, the headwaters of the Qu'Appelle river. This was about 1830.

In the camp of his own people, Flash-in-The-Sky-Boy had to learn to use his own language and to pick up the habits and customs of the band. Naturally he was an object of great interest, for he could now tell them a great deal about the Sioux they had not known before. The Crees laughingly called him "the Sioux Cree" or Nehiyawapot. This came to be accepted as the name of the band for now they had the skills of the two cultures, their own and the Sioux, at their command. To this day the Cree name for Payepot's band is Nehiyawapot. A brother of Flash-in-The-Sky-Boy gave him a nickname, Payepot, which is "a hole in the Sioux" meaning probably that he had made a breach in the secret life of their enemies, the Sioux, and had brought them intimate knowledge of the Sioux way of life. The nickname stuck to the boy and he became known to history as Payepot.

As he grew to manhood he proved to be remarkable in many ways.

Piapot, Cree chief.

He was a famous warrior, a revered Medicine Man, a great horse thief, bringing in many fine horses for the use of the band. And he was also a man of vision and wisdom and was called to sit in the council of the Rattler's tepee, the council of the bravest. In the rain dance he acquired a reputation for magic in rain making.

No one knows when Payepot became a chief but doubtless it was when he was a mature man, at the height of his skill as a hunter and warrior which may have been in the 1840's. If so, he was a chief for more than sixty years.

Abel Watetch

OLD MAN, THE SWEAT LODGE

The sweat lodge is built of willows covered with hides and has in the centre a circle of hot rocks over which water is poured to make steam. The sweat lodge is a sacred rite among all the Prairie people. Phil George, a young Nez Percé, captures this religious significance in the following poem which he wrote while he was a student at the Institute of American Indian Arts.

OLD MAN, THE SWEAT LODGE

"This small lodge is now
The womb of our mother, Earth.
This blackness in which we sit,
The ignorance of our impure minds.
These burning stones are
The coming of new life."
I keep his words near my heart

Confessing, I recall my evil deeds.
For each sin, I sprinkle water on fire-hot stones,
The hissed steam is sign that
The place from which Earth's seeds grow
Is still alive.
He sweats.
I sweat.

I remember, Old Man heals the sick,
Brings good fortune to one deserving.
Sacred steam rises;
I feel my pores give out their dross.
After I chant prayers to the Great Spirit,
I raise the door to the East.
Through this door dawns wisdom.

Bringing in the sweat lodge willows.

Cleansed, I dive into icy waters.
Pure, I wash away all of yesterday.
"My son, walk in this new life.
It is given to you.
Think right, feel right.
Be happy."
I thank you, Old Man, the Sweat Lodge.

Phil George

MOVING THE CAMP

Although men had the power of life or death over their wives and could on occasion be very harsh to the woman who was unfaithful, this story by George Gilles, a Métis who lived with the various Indian tribes of the Prairies around the 1890's, shows that the woman sometimes managed to have things her own way.

At the time of which I write, we were camped in the shelter of the timber, on a little stream that empties into the Red Deer River. The winter had been a fine one, and buffalo were near and numerous all winter. Thousands of buffalo robes had been dressed and thousands of hides made into moccasins and tent leather. Wolves and foxes had been killed by hundreds.

When the thaw set in at springtime, our camp presented a frightful appearance. Carcasses that had been snowed under now came in sight. Scraps of meat, clippings of hide, and tufts of hair lay round everywhere. Everybody wished to leave the winter camp ground and get to some cleaner and nicer spot, but according to the tribal customs, nothing could be done without the consent of the council.

Late one night, the head men met in council, but did not come to a decision about moving the camp till everyone else had gone to sleep. Their resolve was that the camp should be moved, and in view of the temperate state of the weather, and in the interests of cleanliness, very prompt action was decided upon. Very early next morning, before there was any stir about the camp, the camp crier was sent out, making the round of the tepees crying, "The camp must be moved this morning. The young men must not go to hunt or to set their traps till the camp is moved and pitched on the opposite side of the creek."

On hearing this rather unexpected order from the council, there was an immediate commotion in the camp, and everyone was wide awake and astir in a moment or two. There was a general inclination on the part of the people to obey the orders from the council as proclaimed by the crier.

Breaking camp at Belly River, Alberta, July, 1893.

In a short time every tepee was down and being packed up in preparation for moving but one. This one belonged to a woman whose husband had taken another and younger wife in the first part of the winter. He, the husband, with his young wife, lived alongside wife Number One in a tepee of their own. When he saw that his wife Number One had not pulled her tepee down, he insisted on her taking it down right way. This she refused to do, but her husband stood over her with a gun in his hand and gave her to understand that she must pull the tepee down without further delay and prepare to shift camp along with the rest of the tribe. (It will be noticed that the work, as was the Indian custom, was put upon the woman to do.)

When she saw there was no other course open for her, she went to work to pack up her stuff and pull the tepee down. The tepee she rolled up and put on the pony with the pots and kettles on the top. The tepee poles she tied in two bundles and slung to the pack saddle so that the pony could drag them. When all this was done she still had a large bundle to carry. This she knelt down in front of and put the strap that was attached to it on her head, and rose up with the pack on her back, and followed her pony. Her husband followed at her heels.

Just as they were reaching the creek, her husband noticed that the pack on the pony was slipping off to one side, and as his wife was nearer to the pony than he was, he called to her to drop her load and attend to the pony for fear everything should get wet. She accordingly dropped her load on the bank and ran to the pony, which had now reached the creek. Before she could right his load she was waist deep in the creek, so she hung onto the pony till he reached the opposite bank.

When she looked back she saw that her lord and master had taken up the pack she had dropped and was midway in the stream with it on his back. While she was thus taking in the situation, her husband looked up and saw his wife watching him as he bore the burden upon his back in mid-stream. No doubt by this time the reasons for her reluctance at pulling down her tent on such short notice had dawned upon his mind. So, while the wife stood on the bank of the creek looking at him, he deliberately threw the pack into the deepest part of the stream.

Travois.

When the wife saw this, her reserve departed and she yelled to her husband, "He'll drown. Pull him out!" But the husband, standing waist deep in the swift running water, found the whole situation so ludicrous that he almost let the living contents of the bundle drown before he made an effort at rescuing the fast tied bundle. By this time the bundle was a struggling mass of lively "household effects."

It turned out that this woman, with the example of her husband to guide her, had thought that two could play at the game. If her husband could take another wife into his home, she could also receive the attentions of another swain. This man, who in her devotion she had bundled up and packed on her back, was her sweetheart. On this visit he had lingered rather longer than usual and had not yet departed when the proclamation of the crier had aroused the camp so suddenly that he could not leave the lodge without running chances of detection. We have heard of small men who have hidden away in various places, but this particular brave was a tall, strapping fellow.

George Gilles

ADVENTURES OF MY UNCLE

Ohiyesa (Charles Eastman) and his family fled from Minnesota with other members of the Sioux nation in 1895 with the Washechu (white men) hot on their trail. Two years later his father and his two older brothers were betrayed in Winnipeg and for ten years Hakadah (Ohi-yesa's boyhood name) thought they had been killed by white men. He lived those years with his uncle and it is this great hunter who speaks here. Charles' father, who had escaped death, later reclaimed him and took him back to the United States.

My uncle, who was a father to me for ten years of my life, was almost a giant in his proportions, very symmetrical and "straight as an arrow." His face was not at all handsome. He had very quiet and reserved manners and was a man of action rather than of unnecessary words. Behind the veil of Indian reticence he had an inexhaustible fund of wit and humour; but this part of his character only appeared before his family and very intimate friends. Few men knew nature more thoroughly than he. Nothing irritated him more than to hear some natural fact misrepresented. I have often thought that with education he might have made a Darwin or Agassiz.

He was always modest and unconscious of self in relating his adventures. "I have often been forced to realize my danger," he used to say, "but not in such a way as to overwhelm me. Only twice in my life have I been really frightened, and for an instant lost my presence of mind.

"Once I was in full pursuit of a large buck deer that I had wounded. It was winter, and there was a very heavy fall of fresh snow upon the ground. All at once I came upon the body of the deer lying dead on the snow. I began to make a hasty examination, but before I had made any discoveries, I spied the tips of two ears peeping just above the surface of the snow about twenty feet from me. I made a feint at not seeing anything at all, but moved quickly in the direction of my gun, which was leaning against a tree. Feeling, somehow, that I was about to be taken advantage of, I snatched at the same moment my knife from my belt.

"The panther (for such it was) made a sudden and desperate spring. I tried to dodge, but he was too quick for me. He caught me by the shoulder with his great paw, and threw me down. Somehow, he did not retain his hold, but made another leap and again concealed himself in the snow. Evidently he was preparing to make a fresh attack.

"I was partially stunned and greatly confused by the blow; therefore I should have been an easy prey for him at the moment. But when he left me, I came to my senses; and I had been thrown near my gun! I arose and aimed between the tops of his ears — all that was visible of him — and fired. I saw the fresh snow fly from the spot. The panther leaped about six feet straight up into the air, and fell motionless. I gave two good war-whoops, because I had conquered a very formidable enemy. I sat down on the dead body to rest, and my heart beat as if it would knock out all my ribs. I had not been expecting any danger, and that was why I was so taken by surprise.

"The other time was on the plains, in summer. I was accustomed to hunting in the woods, and never before had hunted buffalo on horseback. Being a young man, of course I was eager to do whatever other men did. Therefore I saddled my pony for the hunt. I had a swift pony and a good gun, but on this occasion I preferred a bow and arrows.

The Buffalo Hunt by Francis Kagige

"It was the time of year when the buffalo go in large herds and all the bulls are vicious. But this did not trouble me at all; indeed, I thought of nothing but the excitement and honour of the chase.

"A vast plain near the Souris river was literally covered with an immense herd. The day was fair, and we came up with them very easily. I had a quiver full of arrows, with a sinew-backed bow.

"My pony carried me in far ahead of all the others. I found myself in the midst of the bulls first, for they are slow. They threw toward me vicious glances, so I hastened my pony on to the cows. Soon I was enveloped in a thick cloud of dust, and completely surrounded by the herd, who were by this time in the act of fleeing, their hoofs making a noise like thunder.

"I could not think of anything but my own situation, which confused me for the moment. It seemed to me to be a desperate one. If my pony, which was going at full speed, should step into a badger hole, I should be thrown to the ground and trampled under foot in an instant. If I were to stop, they would knock me over, pony and all. Again, it seemed as if my horse must fall from sheer exhaustion; and then what would become of me?

"At last I awoke to a calm realization of my own power. I uttered a yell and began to shoot right and left. Very soon there were only a few old bulls who remained near me. The herd had scattered, and I was miles away from my companions.

"It is when we think of our personal danger that we are apt to be at a loss to do the best thing under the circumstances. One should be unconscious of self in order to do his duty. We are very apt to think ourselves brave, when we are most timid. I have discovered that half our young men give the war-whoop when they are frightened, because they fear lest their silence may betray their state of mind. I think we are really bravest when most calm and slow to action."

Charles Eastman

RONNIE

Ronald Potts is a Stoney (Assiniboine). He lives on the Alexis Reserve at Glenevis, Alberta, when he isn't away working for a farmer, rancher, or a construction company. He told part of his life story in a film called "Ronnie" from which the following excerpt is taken.

My biggest ambition when I was going to school was writing an Indian dictionary, to write words, Indian words, in the Stoney language — to actually make an alphabet for it. That was one of my biggest ambitions, other than to be a lawyer. When I was a kid I had a way of talking myself out of scrapes. They used to tease me for that. They called me a lawyer and everything like that.

I was very attached to my grandfather. He died when I was seven years old. That came as a great shock to me. When he died I didn't believe it. I thought he was asleep until I actually saw that he was buried. He was a person who never held no grudge against anybody, also he was a person who would help anybody in trouble no matter who it was and also he was fun to be with. He used to tell me stories — old time stories, tribal stories. He used to tell us stories about war (fights they had), passed on from his grandfather, to his father and to him. More or less stuff like when a bird is supposed to help you — or a fish. Those stories used to be very nice to listen to, anyway.

When I was in school it wasn't school I didn't like. In fact, I really enjoyed school. I studied awfully hard to be a model student and succeeded most of the time. When I went to school in the city, I didn't like the way of living in the city. If they would have let us go to school in the country I would have probably stayed in school because I was lost in the city completely. It was quite a change for me being raised in the country then all of a sudden switching to the city where there is lights, cars — I just couldn't get used to that kind of living. I stayed in the city for approximately four months, I couldn't take it. I lived on the main street. Every time it was time to go to bed it was time to get up and go to school. I fell asleep in class a few times. I felt embarrassed about that.

I felt I was caged. I felt like I was captive, I just couldn't take it. I took off about seven or eight times. I played hooky from school and they expelled me. I got a notice saying that I was expelled. By that last time I was getting use to school and had taken off for the last time. I really did take off as a dare — one of the boys told me, "You wouldn't take off again", and as a child, a foolish child, I took off and that was one of my biggest mistakes of my life.

We were out in Goose Lake, and that was the place where my Mom died. My mother was a real kind-hearted person, she was a forgiving sort of person, she was real good with us kids. I think really if more people were like her everybody's children would be more happy. I guess we were out working in the field and my mother came up to where we were working and she brought a lunch for us. She came up with the girls and they were skipping rope and everything and she was having a real good time, I guess on the way back (it was about 8:30 in the evening) she tripped on a stump and she was in child at the time. She had internal injuries I guess. She started bleeding and my father asked if she thought we should get her to a hospital and she said it wasn't serious and asked him to wait and my father went ahead and tried to find a ride for her down at this farmer's place and he asked him if he could take my mother to the hospital and he said no. He didn't come out and say no but he said his car wouldn't start. So we left from there and as soon as we were out of the yard he started his car and was off somewhere, probably to town or something. We went to his neighbour's place and got pretty well the same reception from them so we had to wait for our boss because he had to go to the city and when he came back we told him about it and he said, "Get in and we'll go right away." I guess he realized it was an emergency. He never took time out to start his car or anything he just went in his truck and they left and after Dad came back and I knew that Mom had died. Then he started telling me about it and he was all broken up, crying and stuff like that and he said they had just hit the four lane highway when she started talking to him about the kids — she wanted him to take care of the kids, have them all settled and he was supposed to go to her I guess. I don't know why she said that but I guess she knew she was going away from him and after she finished that she kissed my Dad and I guess she died right in his arms.

Then we went home, we had a funeral. We lived together for a while, that is my two brothers and my father. Then before winter came along when school started my little sisters were put in a residential school that is in Hobbema. They go to school there all year round and they come out for summer holidays and then we went out trapping. That was the only one thing we could do to stay together and when evening came along my father used to pace the room go back and forth and sometimes my brothers had said they had seen him crying in the evening especially just before sundown. I guess he couldn't get over the fact that my mother was dead and they were pretty close because they were two people that must of really loved each other. Wherever my father went my mother was along or where my mother went my father was along. And finally around the middle of February I guess that was about seven or eight months after my mother died he shot himself.

The way it had happened. We were at home or rather out on the trapline. We were having a target practice in the middle of the night at 12:00 at night. I don't know what prompted him to do that. Everybody went inside the cabin, my uncle Frank was there too, my Dad's brother, and they all went in the cabin, Frank, Peter, and Ray. And the old man never came in. We didn't think too much of it at the time but Ray said, "He may be up to something." So he went outside and he saw my father on his knees. He had a gun propped up against his throat and I guess he made the sign of the cross and stuff like that and the last thing Raymond heard the old man say was, "You boys take care of my little boy Gilbert." Gilbert happened to be his pet I guess, and shot himself.

Ronald Potts

THE SPIRIT TRAIL

Mrs. Rowland, a Sioux, does not see the present or future of her people with hope. From her suffering and that of her people comes this beautiful lament.

THE SPIRIT TRAIL

Tall grey and silent they pass sadly by.
Bring with them brooding silence of ache and of need.
Bring with them faint breezes of glory and pride.
 The life! The colours, the joys. The old ways.
 Horses' sides heaving, hoofs crashing and thundering.
 Young warriors, fighting, boasting, and wondering.
 Maidens' dark eyes, laughing and beckoning.
 And the dancing! Oh the dancing, drums beating and beating.

Now all that is left is the cold.
 Red colour of blood, medicine paint and red feeling.
 Blue emptiness, blue coats, blue death like lightning.
 Women keening, hollow and starving.
 Old people freezing, sick and dying.
 And the cold, oh the cold, white death for the women.

Now all that is left is the cold.

Tall grey and cold they pass silently by.
Bring with them the anger, the hate, the distrust.
Bring with them deep sadness for earth's own children.

V. Rowland

Chapter V

Riel, Rebels, and Radicals

In the relative calm of Canadian history there is a bolt of brilliant and radical red — the Riel Rebellion of 1885 and the subsequent execution of Louis Riel in the city of Regina. Eighty-three years later on Wednesday, October 2, 1968, the Prime Minister of Canada, the Honourable Pierre Elliott Trudeau unveiled a statue to that same man in that same city. In his speech the Prime Minister said:

"Both in 1879 in what is now Manitoba, and in 1885 in what is now Saskatchewan, Riel and his followers were protesting against the government's indifference to their problems and its refusal to consult them on matters of vital interest. . . . Today we pay tribute to Louis Riel as a fighter for the rights of his people. Those who share his thirst for social justice should preserve his memory in their hearts."

Cries of outrage have come from many Indians and from many of those who, like Riel, are only partly Indian. Men like Almighty Voice died fighting to preserve a world that was passing. Other men and women have fought just as hard to proclaim a new and better world. Some used the traditional weapons of guns or arrows. Some the more modern weapons of microphone, guitar, television, and newspaper. Who is the hero? Who is the fool? It may be too soon to know but perhaps the Indian rebels of today will help us create a better world tomorrow.

THE QUEEN VERSUS LOUIS RIEL

Louis Riel returned to his home at Red River after ten years study in Montreal and, at the age of twenty-four, organized the Métis of the settlement against the Canadians who were threatening to take over Red River. During 1869-70 when he controlled the colony under a Provisional Government he executed a troublesome agitator named Thomas Scott, and when the three delegates he sent to Ottawa as negotiators arrived there they were arrested under a warrant from Scott's brother. "English-Protestant-Canadians" were enraged by the execution of one of their number by the "Papist Riel", and an army sent to the colony deposed Riel and forced him into hiding.

In 1884 he was living in the United States when Gabriel Dumont, the man who was to become his first lieutenant, searched him out and asked him to lead the Métis and the Indians against the Canadians. The force of changing times made victory impossible and on May 12th Dumont's forces were defeated at Batoche. Louis Riel gave himself up.

A deeply religious man, Riel considered himself a champion of the oppressed and at his trial he made an eloquent plea for understanding. An edited portion of what was said on that fateful day in July 1885 is reproduced for you here.

The trial of Louis Riel in Regina, 1885.

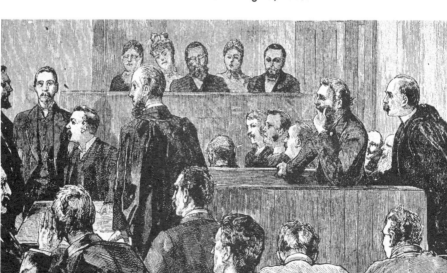

PRISONER: For fifteen years I have been neglecting myself, because I never had much to buy any clothing. The reverend Father André, has often had the kindness to feed my family with a sack of flour: my wife and children are without means, while I am working in the North-West although I am simply a guest of this country, a guest of the Halfbreeds of the Saskatchewan. Although as a simple guest I work to better the condition of the people of the Saskatchewan, at the risk of my life, I have never had any pay. It will be for you to pronounce. If you say I was right, you can conscientiously acquit me, as I hope through the help of God, you will, you will console those who have been fifteen years around me, only partaking in my sufferings; what you will do in justice to me, in justice to my family, in justice to my friends, in justice to the North-West, will be rendered a hundred times to you in this world, and, to use a sacred expression, life everlasting in the other.

CLERK: Gentlemen (of the jury), are you agreed upon your verdict? How say you? Is the prisoner guilty or not guilty?

The jury find the prisoner guilty.

CLERK: Gentlemen of the Jury, hearken to your verdict, as the Court records it: You find the prisoner, Louis Riel, guilty, so say you all.

The Jury answered: Guilty.

A JUROR: Your Honour, I have been asked by my brother-jurors to recommend the prisoner to the mercy of the Crown.

MR. JUSTICE RICHARDSON: I may say in answer to you that the recommendation which you have given will be forwarded in proper manner to the proper authorities.

Louis Riel, have you anything to say why the sentence of the Court should not be pronounced upon you, for the offence of which you have been found guilty.

PRISONER: Yes, Your Honour.

I suppose that after having been condemned, I will cease to be called a fool, and for me it is a great advantage. I consider it as a great advantage. If I have a mission, I say "If" for the sake of those who doubt, but for my part it means "Since," since I have a mission, I cannot fulfill my mission as long as I am looked upon as an insane human being.

I think that I have been called to do something which at least in the North-West nobody has done yet, and in some way I think that to a certain number of people the verdict against me today is a proof that maybe I am a prophet, maybe Riel is a prophet. He suffers for it. Now, I have been hunted as an elk for fifteen years.

I have reasons why I would ask that sentence should not be passed upon me, against me. You will excuse me, you know my difficulty in speaking English, and have had no time to prepare. Your Honour. . . .

The troubles of the Saskatchewan are not to be taken as an isolated fact. They are the result of fifteen years' war. The head of that difficulty lies in the difficulty of Red River. Seven or eight hundred from Canada came to Red River, and they wanted to take possession of the country without consulting the people. True, it was the Halfbreed people. There were a certain number of white pioneers among the population but the great majority were Halfbreeds.

We took up arms against the invaders from the East without knowing them. They were so far apart from us, on the other side of the Lakes, that it cannot be said that we had any hatred against them. We did not know them. They came without notification. They came boldly. We said: Who are they? They said: We are the possessors of the country. Well, knowing that it was not true, we done against those parties coming from the East what we used to do against the Indians from the South and from the West, when they would invade us. The American people were favourable to us; besides, the Opposition in Canada did the same thing and said to the Government: Well, why did you go into the North-West without consulting the people? We took up arms, as I stated, and we made hundreds of prisoners, and we negotiated. A treaty was made. That treaty was made by a delegation of both parties.

Our delegates had been invited three times to meet with those of Canada. How were they received in Canada? They were arrested. To show exactly what is the right of nations, they were arrested. They had not a formal trial, but the fact remains that they were arrested.

I have asked from the Minister of Justice an interview on the fourth of March, and that interview was refused to me. In the month of April, I was expelled from the House. While I was in the woods waiting for my election, Sir John sent parties to me offering me $35,000 if I would leave the country for three years, and if that was not enough to say what I wanted, and that I might take a trip over the water besides and over the world. At the time I refused it. This is not the first time that the $35,000 comes up, and if at that time I refused it, was it not reasonable for me that I should think it a sound souvenir to Sir John? Am I insulting? No, I do not insult. You don't mean to insult me when you declare me guilty, you act according to your convictions. I also act according to mine. I speak true. I say they should try me on this question: Whether I rebelled in the Saskatchewan in 1885.

MR. JUSTICE RICHARDSON: Louis Riel, after a long consideration of your case in which you have been defended with as great ability as I think any counsel could have defended you with, you have been found by a jury who have shown, I might almost say, unexampled patience, guilty of a crime, the most pernicious and greatest that man can commit; you have been found guilty of high treason, you have been proved to have let loose the flood gates of rapine and bloodshed, you have, with such assistance as you had in the Saskatchewan country, managed to arouse the Indians and have brought ruin and misery to many families who, if you had simply left alone, were in comfort and many of them were on the road to affluence. For what you did, the remarks you have made form no excuse whatever, for what you have done the law requires you to answer.

It is now my painful duty to pass the sentence of the court upon you and that is that you be taken now from here to the police guard room at Regina, which is the jail and the place from whence you came, and that you be kept there till the 18th September next, and on the 18th September next you be taken to the place appointed for your execution and there be hanged by the neck till you are dead. And may God have mercy on your soul!

UNIVERSAL SOLDIER

By the time Buffy Sainte-Marie was twenty-four she had already produced two record albums which had sold more than 60,000 copies each. She writes songs as well as singing them and although few of her songs are protest compositions, "The Universal Soldier" is her most famous.

Born on the Piapot [Payepot] reserve, she was adopted by Micmac parents and moved to Maine. She visits her Canadian Cree parents often and when the Diefenbaker Dam was being built in Saskatchewan she gave a benefit concert in Saskatoon to raise funds in an effort to have the sacred Mistasini (rock), 100 miles west of her home reserve moved and saved from the flood.

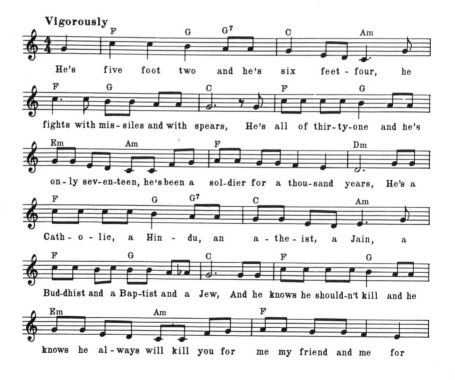

Vigorously

He's five foot two and he's six feet-four, he fights with mis-siles and with spears, He's all of thir-ty-one and he's on-ly sev-en-teen, he's been a sol-dier for a thou-sand years, He's a Cath-o-lic, a Hin-du, an a-the-ist, a Jain, a Bud-dhist and a Bap-tist and a Jew, And he knows he should-n't kill and he knows he al-ways will kill you for me my friend and me for

you, And he's fight-ing for Can-a-da, he's fight-ing for France, he's

fight-ing for the U. S. A., And he's fight-ing for the Rus-sians and he's

fight-ing for Ja-pan, and he thinks we'll put an end to war that

way, And he's fight-ing for Dem-o-cra-cy; he's fight-ing for the Reds, he

says it's for the peace of all, He's the one who must de-cide who's to

live and who's to die and he nev-er sees the writ-ing on the wall,

But with - out him how would Hit - ler have con -
He's the Un - i - ver - sal Sol - dier and he

demned him at Dach - au, With - out him Caes - ar would have stood a -
real - ly is to blame, His or-ders come from far a - way no

lone, He's the one who gives his bod - y as a
more, They come from him and you and me and

(slower)

wea-pon of the war, and with - out him all this kill-ing can't go on,
bro-thers can't you see, this is not the way we put an end to war.

WAR AT FROG LAKE

In June 1931, the Reverend Dr. Ahenakew, the Cree Anglican priest, unveiled a memorial to those who were killed in the community of Frog Lake during the rebellion of 1885. In speaking about the reasons for the battle, Dr. Ahenakew stated that the eight mounds, the graves of the eight who were killed, were evidence of the last attempt of the Indian to register his disapproval of the ever-increasing power of another race in the land. At the time of the war five bands were camped at Frog Lake. All of them had heard rumours of the uprising of the Halfbreeds and were excited by hopes for victory. Many in the camps had long harboured a strong dislike for the white men in the settlement and some were anxious to join the war path.

Dr. Ahenakew went on to describe the fateful day when the white men were killed.

Big Bear has been greatly blamed for all the happenings of 1885 in these parts. After hearing the stories told and thinking them over carefully I have come to the conclusion that he was not responsible for the massacre. It was true he was chief, but when you come to consider that, as such, he was only the leading man with no actually stated powers, you can imagine how easy it was for any reckless spirits to go against his wishes in a time of excitement. At the first shot, standing near the door of the Hudson's Bay Co. store, he gave a loud yell to stop the deed, but it was too late! The Indians were past obeying any voice.

Big Bear.

The day before the massacre, all was quiet. There were preparations for a feast and a dance. Nobody knew that within a few hours there would be trouble. Still there seemed to be an unnatural lull, as if in anticipation of something. Dogs howled every now and again as if they sensed something. The spirit of unrest that was in the West had infected the Indians. They talked about the rebellion. The feast and the dance was held. It was not a war dance, but with so many Indians congregated together, recklessness began to show itself among the young men. Some men have told me they felt the general excitement and restlessness that prevailed. Towards midnight things began to look alarming.

The first act of hostility was the taking of a horse belonging to one of the white men by an Indian. By this time the young men were feeling reckless enough to do anything. Some rode to the mill further west and brought in all the white men from there. Mounted as they were they hurried back to camp at full speed and this had the additional effect of exciting the people. By now it was daylight. All walked to and fro. The more responsible Indians gave advice to the white men, but it was not taken. From the Agency six white people were walking across the yard. The agent would not go. Wandering Spirit, whose wife was the sister of the Indian Agent's wife, advised the agent to go, presumably in hopes of saving him. The agent was a determined man. Wandering Spirit, seeing his good intentions frustrated, repeated his advice. Still the agent remained obdurate. "Once more," said Wandering Spirit, "I ask you to go." Still the agent would not. "Die then," said Wandering Spirit, shooting him dead. The shot had the effect one would naturally expect it to have under the circumstances. The mob spirit took hold and the slaughter began. The white men tried to escape but were shot down as they were overtaken. All was over in a short time. The only white man to escape death was taken prisoner. Two white women were also made captive but given fair treatment.

It was sad for the killed. It was sadder for the slayers. Everything seemed to conspire towards the bringing about of the deed. Had the white men exercised more tact in their dealings with the Indians as did the old Hudson's Bay Co. men before them, the Indians would have been friendly and the deed might never have taken place. The cumulative force of everything that came into touch with the Indians at this time seemed to have worked towards some such thing.

Dr. E. Ahenakew

A PRISONER'S PLEA

When Riel surrendered to the Canadian forces in early May 1885, he was taken to Regina and held there without being allowed visitors until his trial began on July 20th.

His concern for the welfare of his family and his hopes that he would be able to arouse his sympathizers to come to his assistance, led Riel to petition his jailor for the right to write and sell articles about the war.

Superintendent Dean was as anxious to keep Riel out of the news as Riel was anxious to get into the news and the request was not granted.

Portrait of Louis Riel.

A PRISONER'S PLEA

Would the governor
And the Government
Grant me a favour
In my detainment
My wife, my children
Are poor, have no bread
Could I use my pen
In Jail, for their aid.

Grant me to describe
Scenes in the North West
To write on the tribe
Which has help'd me best
Allow me to pass
Word of my morning
When I saw the mass
Of your braves winning.

Ah! perhaps, your press
And your volunteers
Would, in my distress
Buy my reading tears
I would with the price
Get for my children
Half a cup of rice
Or half a chicken.

Sing, O my verses!
Try and earn, in spite
Of my reverses
Yet a gentle bite
Some bread, for my wife,
My dear Margaret
And spare her a strife
With want and regret.

Margaret! I told
You and your father
Before we enroll'd
Our lives together
That my future was
Still clouded with storms
How my career has
Come to its grand forms.

O Captain! I would
write with discretion
And carefully should
I get permission
To work out humbly
The bread that I wish
For my family
The bread of anguish.

Louis Riel

THE OUTLAW

In 1895, ten years after the Rebellion, Almighty Voice, a young Cree giant, killed a steer belonging to a rancher. For this he was arrested and taken to Duck Lake where one of the policemen told him he would be hanged for his crime. Enraged by this threat, Almighty Voice escaped, and for two years the Mounties could not recapture him. Several who tried to do so were shot and killed.

After two years Almighty Voice, his cousin Going Up to the Sky, and his brother-in-law Topean decided to earn a warrior's death and the three of them challenged the entire Mounted Police force. The battle which took place on the One Arrow Reserve is told here by Chief Buffalo Child Long Lance, Cherokee journalist and honorary Blood Chief, decorated for valour during the First World War, and adopted son of Almighty Voice's mother, Spotted Calf.

Indian runners came into our camp and told us that the famous Indian outlaw Almighty Voice had come out of his two years of hiding in the wilderness, and that he was now going to "fight it out" with the Royal North-West Mounted Police, who for twenty-four months had been scouring every nook and cranny of the North-West for his whereabouts.

Scarcely did we think, on that bright day in 1897 when this news reached our camp, that this young Indian, hardly out of his boyhood, was destined soon to make the greatest single-handed stand in all the history of the North American West.

The news of Almighty Voice's sudden reappearance after two years of baffling evasion was received with grave concern at Prince Albert, forty miles away. At midnight the same day twelve mounted policemen under Captain Allan set out on horseback for the Minnechinas Hills. At the same time another mounted police force under Inspector Wilson was dispatched from Duck Lake.

Captain Allan's party, riding past Bellevue Hill the next morning, noticed in the distance three objects moving toward a small thicket of trees. "I see three antelope over there," one of the constables reported. But when they approached closer they were surprised to discern the naked forms of three young Indians, stripped for battle, with their bare, slick bodies glistening in the sun like the smooth brown coat of the antelope.

Captain Allan knew instantly that he had located his quarry, and he gave quick orders to charge.

The three Indian boys stopped dead in their tracks. Almighty Voice stood and waited until the charging Mounties had advanced to good firing range; then he opened up. The first burst of Indian fire brought down the two officers commanding the detachment. Captain Allan's right arm was smashed with a bullet, and Sergeant Raven sagged forward in his saddle with his thigh crushed and dangling uselessly over the side of his horse. Corporal C.H. Hockin now assumed command of the detachment.

Almighty Voice had now counted his fifth "coup" — one killed and four wounded. As the Mounted Police halted to take care of their wounded and reorganize their forces, Almighty Voice and his two companions disappeared into a small thicket, or bluff as it is called in the North-West — a clump of bush about a half-mile through, now famous as the "Almighty Voice Bluff". His people knew that he had selected this bluff in which to make his last, desperate stand against the Mounties, and that he had no thoughts of ever coming out of it alive.

Corporal Hockin's detachment, which stood guard awaiting the reinforcements that had been summoned, was soon joined by the detachment from Duck Lake. That afternoon this combined force was further reinforced by a command consisting of every spare man from the Prince Albert barracks of the North-West Mounted Police.

At six o'clock that evening Corporal Hockin called for volunteers to charge the thicket. Nine mounted policemen and civilian volunteers answered this call.

This was the most disastrous movement of the day. The Indians, perceiving their intention, were on the edge of the thicket awaiting their onslaught. Scarcely had the fringe of the bush been reached when Corporal Hockin received his death wound, a bullet in the chest.

The rush continued, both Indians and raiders firing as fast as their guns would shoot. Ernest Grundy, postmaster of Duck Lake, was the next to fall dead, with a bullet through his heart. An instant later

Constable J.R. Kerr went down to his death with a ball in the chest.

One of the Indian boys, Topean, had been killed on the edge of the brush, and Almighty Voice had received a bullet which shattered his right leg.

Almighty Voice had now counted his eighth "coup".

As the stillness of night crept over the field on that fatal Friday evening, Almighty Voice shouted out of the bluff to the troops:

"We have had a good fight to-day. I have worked hard and I am hungry. You have plenty of food; send me some, and tomorrow we'll finish the fight."

When this message was interpreted to the Mounted Police they were struck with surprise. But it was the Indian's code: fair fight, fair game, no bad feeling in the heart. It may be hard to believe, but Almighty Voice admired the dashing courage of the Mounted Police fully as much as he did that of his two boy companions. The Indian loves the brave, strong-fighting opponent and hates the weak, cowardly adversary.

Early the next morning a crow flew over the thicket in which the two Indians were hiding. "Tang!" went Almighty Voice's gun, and the crow dashed headlong into the bush, to be devoured raw by the hungry Indians. One of the Mounties remarked: "Isn't it queer? That fellow never wastes a bullet — something falls every time he fires."

Almighty Voice's old mother, Spotted Calf, had stood on top of a rise just behind the thicket all night shouting encouragement to her son. Now and then Almighty Voice would answer his mother through the darkness informing her how he was faring.

After two attacks on Friday, he said, he and his remaining boy relative had dug a hole and got into it and covered it over with brush. They were lying under this brush with their deadly rifles poking out to kill anyone who attempted to come into the thicket after them. Two Mounted Police lay dead ten feet from his pit, he said; and he had taken their rifles and ammunition and thrown away his clumsy old muzzle-loader.

"I am almost starving," he said. "I am eating the bark off the trees. I have dug into the ground as far as my arm will reach, but can get no water. But have no fear — I shall hold out to the end."

Excitement had become intense in the surrounding countryside, as all day Saturday fresh troops were arriving on the field from Regina, Prince Albert, and Duck Lake. The whole population of Assiniboia (now Saskatchewan) seemed to have flocked there overnight.

By Saturday evening the field guns were well in place — a 9-pounder and a 7-pounder — and at six o'clock the first shells were sent thundering into the thicket.

The second shot got the range, and the next landed plump into the spot where the fugitives were known to be ensconced.

The heavy barrage of bursting shells lasted for some time. When it finally ceased and every one of the one thousand Mounties and volunteers stood breathless, wondering what had happened to the fugitives, a voice came out of the brush. It was the voice of Almighty Voice. It said:

"You have done well, but you will have to do better."

Darkness settled quickly over the landscape, and a silence as sickening as the whining, thundering shells of a few moments before bore itself into the very souls of the besieging troops. "Men heard one another breathing," one of them once remarked to me. Creeping in behind the thoughts of their own dead comrades came the half-sad realization that tomorrow would spell the eternal end of the two creatures in the bush below, who had partaken of neither food, water, nor sleep during the last three days. Right or wrong, they had displayed a quality which all brave men admire.

One of them also confided to me that he secretly hoped that the Indians would escape during the night and never be heard from again.

No one will ever know what was in the heart and mind of Almighty Voice during that gruesome, black stillness.

At six o'clock the next morning the big guns began belching forth their devastating storm of lead and iron in deadly earnestness. It was obvious that no living thing could long endure their steady beat.

At noon the pelting ceased. At one o'clock volunteers, led by James McKay (later Justice of the Supreme Court of Saskatchewan) and William Drain, decided to make another raid on the bluff. The Mounties themselves had been refused permission to make another raid, owing to their heavy casualties.

On the first rush the volunteers were not able to locate the hiding-place of the Indians. Well, indeed, had they concealed themselves beneath their covering of brush. A second charge, however, brought them upon the gun-pit.

Here, lying in the brush-covered hole, was the dead body of Almighty Voice.

Chief Buffalo Child Long Lance

THE BEAVER

Duke Redbird, the young Ojibway from Ontario's Bruce Peninsula who runs an Indian culture centre in Toronto believes that: "There never will be an improvement in Indian-white relations in Canada until there is a psychological revolution on the part of all Canadians. It is simply not possible to make progress under the present segregated system".

In "The Beaver" he makes it quite clear that he does not believe the Indian is the only one who needs to change.

THE BEAVER

See how the beaver,
Works all night, without light
In the darkness

He builds his dam
Limb and branch, mud and sand
Higher, stronger, greater dam

From dusk till dawn
His toil goes on, and on

Then tomorrow, you will see
a bubbling stream

Become a pond, and later on
A stagnant lake

And all the creepy, crawly creatures
Will crawl down, to make a home
Within that putrid pond

With turtle, snake, frog and crab,
These neighbours now the beaver will have

But
The deer, bear, lynx and fox,
Raccoon, wolf, moose and hawk

Will move far away
To find a place the beaver hasn't been

Where clear, cold, clean water still flows
Living, Laughing, Tumbling Liquid Life

Waterfalls, brooks and streams
These are highways for life's dreams.

My son,
Do not become a beaver,
And build for yourself a dam

For this is what the whiteman does
With brick and stone and sand

Till his mind is like that lake
Filled with weird wicked wretches
That give no peace.

Then he cries to his creator
In desperation

Please God, my God, deliver me
From Damnation.

Duke Redbird

THE HAVES AND HAVE NOTS

Dr. Howard Adams, Associate Professor of Education at the University of Saskatchewan, is also an author, lecturer, and champion of Indian and Métis rights. His ancestors worked with Riel in the Provisional Government of Manitoba and Dr. Adams is justly proud of his Métis heritage. In this excerpt from his unpublished novel, Dr. Adams draws on his experiences as a boy in rural Saskatchewan where the "haves" did not always share with the "have nots".

Leo walked past the little town of LaRoche. He noticed the Lamarouxs pull onto the highway from the side in their blue Pontiac; they headed in his direction. Lamarouxs were the storekeepers of La-

Roche, and were actually rich. They were outstanding Catholics, for they gave a lot of money to the Church. Father Carrier was their very good friend. They had one of the few houses in LaRoche that was not built of log and mud; it was beautiful, even inside. It had separate rooms inside. Leo had seen it when he called for Jean sometimes. She was the servant girl for the Lamarouxs. Although they never allowed him beyond the front door, Leo thought they were pretty nice to allow him to call for Jean. Often, he had to stand and wait, as Jean frequently had to work overtime.

The Lamarouxs did not associate with the half-breeds, except strictly on business. Leo didn't really like them because they were not very friendly with the Métis, and yet they were getting rich at the expense of the hardwork of the half-breeds. Everybody knew that old man Lamaroux bought cordwood from the Métis for one dollar a cord and paid in groceries that were probably priced high. Then next year he would sell the same wood for three and four dollars a cord, without even touching it. But Leo's relatives were out in the woods before daybreak in forty below weather cutting cordwood. It would take one whole day for one man and a team of horses to make a cord of wood — for one measly dollar of groceries.

And yet these same Lamarouxs were the upper class of LaRoche. "Fils de vipère" "And they're too damn nice for me" grumbled Leo. He was tempted to throw a handful of dirty mud through the open window so that it would splatter all over that phony old Mrs. Lamaroux who acted like a queen. Boy, oh, boy, that would really be fun, thought Leo. She always has her mouth open, maybe he could throw some muck right in her gullet. Let her taste some of God's soil where the half-breeds have to sweat their guts out. Leo quickly picked up a big handful of gooey mud and squeezed it vengefully.

"Baptême" the damn window was closed. He flung it against the fence with all his power of hostility.

Dr. Howard Adams

THE WHITE YUM-YUM TREE

Lloyd Caibaiosai is a mild-mannered young man with a deep resonant voice. An Ojibway from Spanish River, Ontario, Lloyd has startling ideas as well as a sonorous voice and when he speaks people listen.

Here is part of a speech he made to a group of young intellectuals at Glendon College, York University, Toronto.

The white middle-class view, compounded of self-righteousness and paternalism, leads naturally enough to the unbreakable habit of talking about "them" and "us". Thus whites glide smoothly to the conclusion that "we" will somehow rule "them". Right, Great White Father?

This brings me to a proposition which is the key to my understanding of the situation. I offer it tentatively even though I am convinced it is valid. If it is, it makes all of our present difficulties trifling and we have before us a problem of statecraft whose dimensions cannot now be imagined.

"The proposition is that racial integration in Canada is impossible."

I set forth this proposition without qualification. There are no hidden unlesses, buts, or ifs in it. I shall not deny that in some remote future integration may come about. But I do not see it resulting from the actual present trends and attitudes in Canadian society. It can only be produced by some event overturning these trends. There is no denial in this proposition that there will be a steady betterment in the material situation of Indians.

My proposition is sad. My proposition, in short, smashes the liberal dream. It eliminates the democratic optimistic claim that we are finding our way to a harmonious blending of the races. It changes the words of the marching song to "We Shall Not Overcome", or was that "Overrun"?; for what was eventually to be overcome was hostility and non-fraternity, between Indian and White. My proposition dynamites the foundations of the Indian-Eskimo Association, and similar organizations. It asserts that 'Indian Reserve, Canada', and 'Whitetown, Canada' for all practical purposes and with unimportant exceptions, will remain separate social communities.

I am not sure, but it may also mean Indiantown will become a separate political community.

The proposition would seem to place me in the camp of the bigots and locate me with the hopeless, also probably the racists. It puts at ultimate zero the efforts of the tough and high-minded who are giving their lives to the dream of equality among men.

Yet I am convinced that integration in Canada is a sentimental not a doctrinal, idea. We came to the idea late in Canadian history, and it disappears readily from the rhetoric of politics — though not from the list of sacred democratic aims — at the first sign of indocility. The vast fuss of improvement in Indian communities is not aimed at integration. Few are afflicting us any longer with such a tiresome lie. All these measures are primarily aimed at the prevention of civic commotions, secondarily at assuaging the conscience of Whitetown, and finally helping the Indians tell the story.

The country of Canada is a white man's country conducted according to White customs, and White laws for White purposes. I would not even argue that Whites should not run the country for their own interests, but they can't see that racial integration is one of these interests, except in perilous self-deceit. Whites *like* Indians so long as they theselves are not disturbed by Indians. Whites have no objection to bettering the Indians' lives so long as it does not cost much, and as long as it leads to the continuance of Indian Reserve and so does not present the threat of genuine integration at any level. The White condition for Indian betterment is, to put it simply, separation.

Why is it so hard for Whites to say clearly that they do not want Indians or Blacks living among them and sharing their world? There must be dozens of reasons playing on one another. One, I suppose, is that they are ashamed to admit they do not subscribe, after all, to a glorious myth. Another is the Christian message that binds them to brotherhood. But as something in their understanding of Christianity made possible the acceptance of slavery, it continues to make possible the shunning of Indians as less worthy than themselves. Often enough this is accompanied by an aching conscience.

Another reason, I suppose, is that after 476 years Indians are still strangers to Whites. It is a rare white man who is really acquainted with an Indian. Almost as though arranged by Whites.

A commanding reason, I would guess, is to be found in the mystique of progress, in the belief that by nature everything must somehow improve all the time. Thus the present degradation of Indians can be waved aside by referring to better things to come, as come they must to the deserving, perhaps in another century or two or three.

In giving up on integration I am not giving up on the Indians but on the Whites. White attitudes are the problem. Sadly enough, there is only one place where we have registered even a mild success: we have more or less integrated poverty. The liberal view is that patience and persistence will in the end perform the miracle. The enemy is ignorant. Whitetown's resistence, accordingly, is temporary-stubborn perhaps but penetrable by knowledge and association.

Let me put forward the more general testimony in support of my proposition, the race situation is marked by growing expression of distrust, hate, and fear on the part of both Indians and Whites; growing disillusionment throughout all the reserves; increasing belligerency of young Indians and their leaders; increasing impatience of our Dad — Whitey; growing isolation of the Indian middle class who have made it; growing uselessness of treaties between Indians and Whites as Indian demands become more basic and White resistance more determined.

The outside agitator is Whitetown itself. It is more important to recognize that separation-not-integration is the way it has always been. The fostering of the illusion that integration is an achievable goal is bad enough in its effects on Indians, some of whom may still entertain a vision of their children foregathering in total equality under the White yum-yum tree. But the illusion is sinister in its likely consequence for Whites. By engaging in it they are leaving themselves unprepared for the grand finale.

What is necessary is the development of a Canadian democratic system which, in itself, allows men to be equal and live in peaceful coexistence, but maintains the existence of two or three viable separate societies.

Lloyd Caibaiosai

Chapter VI

On the Edge

The huge lonely land of Canada's north marks the edge of the Indian world and the beginning of the barren lands — a world so harsh that the edge of hunger and cold is just beyond the door.

The northern people have lived on the edge for hundreds of years and know how to survive and love it. They are the Kutchin, Nahani, Sekani; the Tsesaut, Tahltan, and Tagish; the Hare, Dogrib, and Slave; the Yellowknife, Chipewyan, and Cree; and in the east beyond Hudson's Bay, the Mistassini Cree, the Montagnais, and Naskapi.

It is a hard land but an exciting one. It is the land of caribou herds of a thousand head; the land of Canada goose flocks so large they darken the sky. It is the land of flower-filled summers where the sun becomes a constant companion and *the people* sleep only in snatches. It is the land of contrast, of extremes.

The people have always known it to be a world of wealth. American and Canadian sportsmen, oil men, miners, and tourists are only now discovering some of the secrets of the north.

ME'JO TALKS TO HIMSELF

In the land of the Naskapi and the Montagnais food is scant. The bear is a prized catch. It is not a willing victim, however, and the hunter will probably require assistance.

Simon Rafaël of the Lake St. John Band describes here how his people learned to make use of the sweat lodge to help them in their hunt.

Me'jo always talks to himself. He once went along a small lake and saw beaver tracks. "Oh, what a lot of beaver! I'll have to eat some." Finally, he found one asleep on the shore and went up to it. "Ah! a dead one. I'll roast him." So he tied his hunting sack to its neck to mark it and went to make a roasting stick.

While he was gone the beaver awoke and jumped up and then dived for the water with the sack. Me'jo saw him and said, "Ah! There's another beaver. I will get him and then I'll have two." But when he saw the beaver with the sack on its neck, he called for him to come back and give him back his sack. But the beaver only laughed and dived, with a whack of his tail. And so Me'jo wandered along the shore talking to himself again; soon he saw other tracks. "Ah! Here is a nice one; he is dead." Then he saw an otter asleep, and went up to it and grabbed it by the chest, feeling to see how fat it was. This tickled the otter and he laughed. "What are you going to do with me?" he asked. "Eat you," Me'jo answered. Then the otter jumped up and dived into the lake. Then Me'jo went upon the big mountain and suddenly found a bear. The bear jumped up, and Me'jo said, "What are you going to do?" "Eat you," said the bear. "Oh! Wait awhile. Don't do that yet. I came here to play, so let's do it first." The bear agreed to this. So Me'jo built a cabin for a sweat lodge and heated stones to put into it. Then he entered the sweat lodge and showed the bear where to go. Said he to the bear, "Here is where I sit, and you sit there."

So they went in and Me'jo began singing. The stones threw off great heat. Soon the bear was overcome with the heat and fell over dead.

Then Me'jo cooked him and got his meal.
(This is the origin of the sweat lodge which is used among the Montagnais to call the bears so that they can be killed.)

Simon Rafaël

From NASKAPI, by Frank G. Speck, Copyright 1935
by the University of Oklahoma Press.

THE SPELL OF THE WINDEGO

Mr. Gordon Moore is a Cree. He started going blind when he was in elementary school and as a result his formal education stopped at the end of grade three. This remarkable self-educated man, now in the Sudbury Institute for the Blind, has "written" many poems about the James Bay country as he remembers it.

THE SPELL OF THE WINDEGO

We love the glow where winter snow
Is piling white and deep
Where Northern lights on frosted night
Keep children from their sleep.

Come out to play, they seem to say,
The hour is rich and bright.
And laughter rings and spins and sings
In children's ears at night.

We are the children of the sky
We laugh and play and dance.
We Windego are full of fun
Come join our magic dance.

With trailing green and red between
And blinding yellow bars
We heed the tune of mellow moon
And dance beneath the stars.

Each little one is running wild
And singing glad refrain!
Let children be where they may see
Those Northern lights again!

Gordon Moore

BONANZA

*The fabulous Klondike gold rush was started by three Tagish Indians
and their white relative. Kulsin — Patsy Henderson — was twenty years*

old when his brother Charles Henderson (Dawson Charlie), his uncles James Mason (Skookum Jim) and George Carmack discovered gold on Rabbit Creek. They called their find "Bonanza". It made them rich and opened up the Yukon to swarms of white prospectors.

When he was living in Carcross, Mr. Patsy Henderson gave the following account of the discovery that changed the North.

This is the Klondike story now. I am going to tell Klondike story. Here is the man (pointing to picture) who found the first gold. That man's name is Dawson Charlie and he find gold in '96 the 17th of August. He is my brudder and his pardner, Skookum Jim, my uncle. Another pardner, George Carmack (he is a white man, George Carmack) and myself. Four of us, now these people all die excepting me. The time we find gold in the Klondike — just a kid, I am old man now.

I want to tell you a little story about George Carmack. George when he came to this country about '88, no white man here that time; no store, just Indian around here, but white man way down river; not in here. So that George Carmack come from outside Chilkoot Pass. When he come this he married Skookum Jim sister, my aunt. He stay around here with Indians. First year he didn't understand the way Indian live; when he stay with Indian two years he understand. At that time we don't work for nobody, we work for ourselves. He don't work for nobody. He stay around here five years. He got tired around here and wife and he went down Yukon river. When he went down he said he would not come back for two years. He never came back for two years. We miss him. We go down looking for him — Charlie, Skookum Jim and me — built little rowboat, and we go through Canyon to Whitehorse in rowboat and we row the boat all way down the river. No machine; all hand work. We rowed down the Yukon from Tagish. Two weeks time. When we come down Klondike we find him, George Carmack. He stay among the Indians on the Klondike. We told him we come down to look for you. He tell us too bad you fellows look for me long ways and he tell us we can't come back till winter time. (Till river froze over.) So we stay and put feesh trop in water on the Klondike river. Feesh for winter — feesh for dogs. After a while he (George

Carmack) tell us one man he come up the river before you fellows; that man he told me he found gold last fall away back and that is where he went again, that man. That man is named Bob Henderson. He is a white man; we haven't seen him but George saw him. George tell us let us go look for that man; maybe he found lots of gold. He tell us like that, so we go look for him, Charley, Skookum Jim, and George Carmack — three people look for Bob Henderson. That is time they find gold, but I stay home in camp on Klondike. I look after feesh trop and dogs in camp. Three people leave Klondike own camp and start off up the creek; but the first gold found eight miles from camp. Dawson Charlie found 10¢ nugget (little pin head).

He don't find in creek; find on side hill on slide on top of rock. So we went up creek; we see gold, we pan it; but at same time they look for Bob Henderson, and find him away back, maybe forty miles from the Klondike. Bob Henderson — 2-3 days trip we find him. Bob Henderson has got a creek and he got a little gold; he stay there and he is alone. But those three people stay at Bob Henderson's camp one night; the next day they turn back. But they come back different creek and they see gold again. Everytime they come down a little ways then they see gold, but they look for good large place, nobody bodder, they pan; so when they come down half way creek they take a rest on top of bank and one man go down creek to get drink of water. Skookum Jim go down to creek for drink of water. When he took drink of water he see gold. When he got through drinking he call, "George come down here; bring down shovel and gold pan and we try here". When George come down to the creek, "Look, George, look at gold on rock" — but George says that is gold. But gold on creek he pan. First pan 50¢ gold he panned. He tried a little bit above; he found lots of gold. A little below lots of gold. Twenty minutes panned $5 gold, coarse gold. Then George say, "I think we have a good place; I am staking claim". Staked claim for three people. When they staked claim they named creek, Bonanza. First creek to be found in Klondike. Lots of creek after a while. Same evening they came back to camp. When they come back they got gold and George Carmack he weighed, they had small gold scales; he says $5 worth of gold; 50¢ per pan average. When I see the gold first just like I don't care because I no savvy; I never see gold before; now I like

Mining on Bonanza Creek, 1898.

to see gold all the time (laugh). Next day we go down to Forty Mile to record the claim. Forty Mile was mining camp before '98 and recorder office there. So we record claim. We come back again. Go down one day come back two days. When we get up to camp on Klondike we move the camp up the creek up to Bonanza so when we get up there we build ten feet sluice box. Cut with axe; we start work on first day September, worked for three weeks. In three weeks time we took out gold $1450. At that time very cold; we cannot stand it no longer. We go down to 40 mile for winter camp. We took gold in store; we tell people we took out this gold in three weeks' time — $1450. That is the time the big rush start. No one stay home, everybody go up. The big rush start to come up the river two years steady; winter time, summer time, every day somebody come. After two years '98 big rush start, from out over Chilkoot Pass. When big rush starts in '98 around here, there were 20,000 people around Bennett Lake and Tagish Lake. At same time they start railroad from Skagway; that time no bulldoze; all hand work; shovel work. When railroad come this country around here, everything come; horses, policemen, everybody come.

Patsy Henderson

RABBIT HUNTING

John Tetso was a Slavey. He made his living by trapping. He was once the chief of his band and he wrote a column for the Fort Simpson Catholic Voice. *In 1964 when he was at his Willow River camp, 110 miles north of his Fort Simpson home, he got pneumonia and died before his family could get him to hospital. He was forty-three. After his death Father Henri Posset, O.M.I. published Mr. Tetso's writings in a book called* Trapping Is My Life.

Way back in 1942, I bought my first .22 rifle from Herb Kerr, a white trapper, in town. Day after we got home, I took my shooting iron down the mouth of Trail creek and took it all apart, examined it, put it back together. Then I loaded it with shells, pumped one into the firing chamber, aimed it and pulled the trigger. It worked well.

Next day a gang of us guys went rabbit-hunting. I didn't know how to call rabbits, so, I asked one of my friends. He said that I could learn it from the rabbits. I asked him how and he told me. So I took my gun and walked into the bush. I did not go far and I ran into a litter of young baby rabbits. I chased one that seemed never stops, but finally I caught it. The little rabbit started crying, producing long kissing-like sound. Soon, an adult rabbit came running out of the woods, circling me. Very soon, another one, and then another one. Three rabbits and I got two out of three.

I let the little rabbit go, walked a little way up and called, making sounds just like that little rabbit. Sure enough, rabbits came running from all directions, five of them. I put two of them in my pack.

All morning, I walked through the woods. Every so often I stopped to call and picked some, till I had quite a load, then, I went back to the starting point to find the gang all there, feasting on rabbits.

Nearly every day we go rabbit-hunting back in those days. Rabbits were plentiful then. This is in the month of June of that year. On one of these hunts, Frank Cli got lost, and stayed in the bush for more than twelve hours. Wind was blowing hard and we all split up in pairs, walking through the woods, calling for Frank. Comes ten o'clock in the evening, but no Frank, so we went home, thinking maybe he found an old trail and went home on it. When we got home, nobody had seen him, so back we went. We looked and searched, covering about four miles. We worked all afternoon, all night till eight o'clock next morning when we went back to the river, tired. We made tea and had something to eat and were ready to go again, when we saw someone coming along the shore. When he came up, it was Frank alright, tired. Ten o'clock we went home, and to bed I went.

Well to some of the readers these things that I do seem rather cruel; I know that too, but I don't have a warehouse full of grub with me all the time, and I got to get it from the bush.

John Tetso

CONVERSATIONS WITH MARIA MICHANO

"Maria" is a combination of four Ojibway girls from Northern Ontario. They had a teacher, J. McLeod, who loved to listen to them talk about their world. He thought their poetry was great and wrote it down so that we could enjoy it too.

MY DOG

I got a dog for me
and he a jellybean dog
and look stupid

For once my father
try to take away
the food
and the dog snarl
and dive at my father.
My father said,
it was good to have a dog
but not one
so bad as this.

THE DENTIST

One time I tell you
the dentist came
to town
All the kids scared.
I feel like I have
no bones in me.
He says,
get on the chair.
Colatt was there.
I close my eyes.
Then he say,
brave girl, see you next time.
I laugh then,
Colatt was next.

THE HUNT

Once my brother and me
for walk in the land.
He laugh.
He have his gun
look for animal.
A bird in the tree
make the noise
and my brother turn quick
and smile
and I laugh and laugh.
My brother is get mad
for he say, no animal
with a laughing girl
in the land.

KIDS IN TOWN

Why kids in town
for shout?
Shout? Shout? Shout?
I don't shout for all.
When I need for shout,
I can,
but I talk soft
and watch
the teacher ear
in our class.

J. McLeod

THE FACE OF A THIEF

Phil Thompson is a Slavey from Fort Simpson whose career has included being a pilot with the R.C.A.F., a university student, Director of the Edmonton Indian Friendship Centre, Band Manager for the Hay Lakes Band, and candidate for the New Democratic Party. Like many educated Indian people he has devoted his life to assisting other Indians. He included the following true anecdote in a speech he made in Regina in 1965.

There was once a wise old Indian man who had heard of some parents who did not bother to send their children to school.

So this wise old man paid a visit to the parents and upon arrival made the statement, "I wanted to see what the face of a thief looked like, and now I see it."

Of course, the parents were set back and the father said, "We are not thieves, we are honest people. If by mistake we have taken something that is not ours, we will gladly return it."

The old man replied, "It is not something you can see, not something you can hear or feel, nevertheless it is something very real. In this day of ours, there are rights and opportunities that belong to us and our children, especially to the children. There are opportunities of going to school. These opportunities belong to the children and they need them. They need them to make their way in life. And any parent who does not ensure that his children get these opportunities is robbing them of their rights. I will say no more."

This wise old man left the same day. However, the next morning all the children of this family were at school.

This is what I mean when I speak of responsibility. For we rob our children when we do not ensure that they get all the opportunities for education.

Phil Thompson

KLEVITI DEFEATS THE ESKIMO

Kleviti was a hero of the Chandlar Kutchin who lived in the time of Johnny Frank's grandparents. The small but fantastic Kleviti's adventure is described by Mr. Frank, a resident of Arctic Village, Alaska.

The Chandlar Kutchin were often at war, mostly with the Eskimos, or Huskies, as we called them. The bravest fighter of the Chandlar tribe was a little man called Kleviti who lived near the site of the present Arctic Village. His daughter, Klevi by name, was a contemporary of my father and mother.

One time Kleviti and his family, together with two other men, were camped on the far side of the range west of Arctic Village. They were living in two conical tents of caribou skin, one belonging to Kleviti and his family and one belonging to the two men. Since there was no timber about the camp, it was possible to see a great distance.

One day a large band of Eskimos came up one creek while a second band came up another. They came together at Kleviti's camp. The latter gave no sign of fear, but sat calmly in his tent. When some of the Eskimos went to the creek to get some water, Kleviti went down and watched them, but he did not drink himself.

When one of the Chandlar Kutchin in the other tent lay down to sleep, Kleviti warned his companion to keep an eye on the Eskimos. Kleviti had a double-ended knife of soft iron, which he carried up his sleeve. Finally some of the Eskimos came into Kleviti's tent, taking places on each side of him. One of them gave him an arrow as a present. Suddenly the Eskimos by his sides grabbed for Kleviti, but he was too quick for them and killed them both, one with each end of his knife. Two more Eskimos were standing by the entrance of the tent, and others were outside. Kleviti leaped through the door, stabbing each of the two Eskimos in the neck, and then ran right through the group outside.

The Eskimos then seized the sleeping Indian in the other tent and ripped open his belly with a knife. When Kleviti came running up, they shot arrows at him but did not hit him. When their arrows were exhausted, Kleviti killed these Eskimos with a short spear. Other Eskimos came running up, but as soon as they had exhausted their arrows they ran away. At the start of the fight Kleviti's son and daughter had taken refuge under a low bank. Kleviti's wife had been wounded by an arrow, but not until after she had killed one Eskimo. Kleviti continued running, jumping, and dodging arrows, some of which fell near his children. Finally only a few Eskimos remained, the rest having retreated. Kleviti now took his own bow and arrows, and the Eskimos cried in fright for they were afraid of him.

In the meantime one Eskimo crept up behind the bank and let drive an arrow from close range. At the twang of the bow string Kleviti jumped aside so deftly that the arrow merely grazed his thumb. The Eskimos ran across the stream, but Kleviti followed them, picking them off one by one. When he had used up all his arrows, he turned to his spear and his club. He shot his last Eskimo off the top of a small bank, using the same arrow that the latter had given him as a present. Kleviti continued his pursuit while his children watched from their hiding place. Only five of the enemy remained. They had but a few arrows left so they dodged in and out of the brush. As often happens when men fight, the sky suddenly became dark, and a heavy fog drifted in. Kleviti had no wish to follow the enemy farther into the brush, so he returned to his family. On the way back he picked up many spent arrows and, when he arrived at camp, he built a fire with them. He kept guard all night but the surviving Eskimos did not return.

The next morning he removed an arrow which had pierced both breasts of his wife. He cleaned her wound by tying a piece of wet caribou skin to a string and pulling this through. That night he heard a man crying near the spot where he had shot the Eskimo leader. The next morning he went to this place and found the man dead. The Eskimo's clothes were decorated with many big beads. Kleviti took these and then returned with his family to his camp near the present Arctic Village.

Kleviti had an elder brother called Herilu who lived down the river from Arctic Village. Herilu was very wealthy, but he was not a warrior like his brother.

The next year Kleviti and his brother went back to the scene of the fight. There is a glacier near this place and the Indians met a large party of Eskimos here. The latter were determined to revenge themselves on Kleviti. Because Herilu was a wealthy man rather than a warrior, they told him of their intentions, but Herilu advised the Eskimos that if any harm came to Kleviti he would make presents to all the Chandlar Kutchin warriors and thus organize a war party that would wipe out the Eskimos.

Because of this threat the Eskimos gave up their idea of revenge. Instead they engaged in friendly contests of skill with Kleviti, using the glacier as a playing field. First, all the Eskimos tried to lay their hands on Kleviti, but no one could catch him. Then they piled three of their sleds on top of each other, but Kleviti was able to jump over the entire pile. Next, they played "football" on the glacier, and Kleviti outplayed them all. Following these games, they all decided to camp there together for the winter. They became good friends and agreed never to fight each other again. Herilu had many wolverine skins with him and he traded these to the Eskimos.

Johnny Frank

NEWS FROM OLD CROW

Edith Josie is a Loucheux and she comes from Old Crow, a town that is 120 miles south of the Arctic Ocean and eighty miles north of the Arctic Circle. Miss Josie writes the news and sends it to the Whitehorse Star. *She wasn't trained for the job; she didn't even apply for it. Once she was chosen, however, she sent in the facts as she saw them and she wrote them down in her own style of English. Miss Josie did so well that her news bulletins appeared in* Life, *the* Weekend

Magazine, *and on the* CBC. *She now has fans in all parts of the continent.*

January 3

Women dog race held today. Nine teams was in the race. Sorry, the time sheet is lost. It was tack up on the post and the kids have torn it off. Only four times remember is first two teams and middle two teams.

Mrs. Clara Tizyah took first place with the time of eight min. 13 sec. Clara is using Paul Ben Kassi team and look as though Clara made better time than Paul so must be Clara is better musher than Paul.

Alice Frost took second place with time nine min. 15 sec. Bertha Frost took third place time nine min. 55 sec. Also Helen Charlie, Sarah Kay, Ethel Frost, Margaret Njootli.

Annie Nukon was in the race but didn't make it. Cause she had little trouble with her team she came home on the other trail.

January 21

Since Jan. 20 it start to be sunshine and sure look beautiful. No caribou and lots of them got no meat and no grub and lots of them are hungry. When it's nothing to eat and it's sure bad for big family. Mr. Chief Charlie Peter he sure had big family and he had about 10 kids and himself and his wife. They were 12 in his house. They really got nothing no meat.

May 18

I went to Mr. Netro store and I ask him how much rat skin he get and he told me how much he get.

Since February March April and May he got about 20,447 rat skins from the boys in Old Crow. If rat house is good they would killed more but not very good. Cause some rat house is frozen and what is good to set trap for caribou eat the rat house and spoil it.

The caribou is bad for eating rat house when there are no grass and they have to eat rat house. This is why it is hard to get rat this spring. So some boys will go to work at camp. I hope they don't get fire and work steady.

July 28

I been to Inuvik and sure lots of car. Old Crow no car also no airport and phone. These three should be in Old Crow. If these thing in our small town be big surprise for people. Not much fish here this summer.

August 22

Morning around 11 a.m. Peter Benjamin the fire catch him across the River. Those police they tie their dogs other side of river and they always cook dogs feed. So it is rain all night and the wood is wet so Peter Benjamin put gas on wood and he light the fire and fire catch his clothes and he run to river and he just go into water and fire is out. When first thing fire catch him he was holler and someone hear his voice and few motor boat went to him.

September 28

Mr. Peter Moses has been doing lots of work when he alive on this earth. He was happy old man and friendly with anybody even with the white people. So I know everybody will miss him but hope he will have a good rest. He was very kind to the kids most and all the kids like him. When he sees the boys and girls, he talk silly and laugh.

Edith Josie at the *Whitehorse Star.*

When someone make feast he make speech everyone like because he make everyone laugh.

And when the dance is on, he always make jig with his wife. He always make double jig with the girls. He was born on the American side and the year he was born is 1882. I hear he married in 1901. On September 28, he came back from upriver because he spit blood but he was very good and he's not sick. So no one know he was going to die. While that he pass away sure everybody surprise for him.

They make him chief in Old Crow in 1936 and he was chief for 18 years. When he was chief, he sure did a nice job and he always make feast and dance. His wife, Mrs. Myra Moses, she feel happy and all the members of St. Luke WA is making feast for her. Everybody is nice to her and they work for her to make her happy.

All the men make coffin for him and they going to dig ground for him on Oct. 2.

They will have funeral service on Oct. 3. Everybody will go to service and the graveyard. That much we miss him. Some women make a beautiful flowers for his graveyard. They will have English and Indian hymn and prayer. Even the school kids will go to service so will have English hymn for him. If the weather is clear some people will fly in to the funeral. From Inuvik, Roy Moses will come to see his grandfather. He stay in Inuvik for making school and he was working there so he will try and come to see his grandfather.

October 10

They see caribous on mountain and the snow is on mountain. Sure look like winter.

Those carpenter and the electric are sure busy every day.

They just call Old Crow town and they should say Old Crow is town now because everyone had lights and lights is on the street and sure look different as before. Soon it get dark the lights is on. Sure look very good.

Edith Josie

Chapter VII

The Council of the Three Fires

Rivalry over fur, payments taken in whiskey, and wars with the wrong allies undermined the great Ojibway. One of the largest nations north of Mexico, at the peak of their power they controlled almost all the territory from the Ottawa River to Lake Manitoba and south of the Great Lakes into what is now the United States.

As a defence against their enemies three of the four Ojibway tribes (the Saulteaux, the Ottawa and the Potawatomi) formed a confederacy known as the Council of the Three Fires. A fourth tribe, the Mississauga, occupied Manitoulin Island.

The Ojibway role as middleman in the early fur trade brought them into alliance with the fur-hungry French. When the French were conquered by the English the Ojibway were defeated as well, in spite of the brilliant general Pontiac, war chief of the Ottawas.

Not only were the Ojibway involved in the white man's wars but they also had to defend themselves from both the Hurons and the Iroquois who were eager for their share of the rich fur traffic. The Saulteaux of the far west under Chief Peguis formed an alliance with the Selkirk settlers and found themselves defending the Scottish immigrants from other Indians.

The Ojibway's constant battles sapped their strength, left them scattered and poorly prepared for the changes that were to come. Although defeated many times, they were never crushed.

Today, Ojibway men and women are active in almost every aspect of Canadian life.

Tom Peyash fishes for whitefish, pickerel, and pike, using a gill net. His home, Grassy Narrows, is just north of Kenora near the Manitoba border.

WESAKACHAK AND THE BEAVER

Jackson Beardy collected legends from both the Cree and Ojibway in Manitoba. These people often tell the same story about "the Trickster" whom the Cree call Wesakachak and the Ojibway call Nanabozho.

The beavers downstream were observing Wesakachak sleeping by the shoreline.

"Let's go wake him up," one of them piped up.

"Okay, you're brave, Broadtail, go wake him up. You're the daring one."

Broadtail swam quietly beside Wesakachak's face and slammed his tail on the water splashing the water on his face. Wesakachak instantly awoke bubbling and gurgling and was in time to see where the beaver was. Jumping into the water, he grabbed Broadtail by the tail and dragged him ashore.

"Ha! I have the last laugh this round," Wesakachak said as he beat the beaver. The beaver automatically played dead. He used the rope from his tobacco pouch and fixed the beaver in such a way he could

124   I AM AN INDIAN

carry him on his back into the bush. On the way, several times the beaver on Wesakachak's back purposely slapped his face with his tail. Soon Wesakachak's face was beaten raw but all this time he thought the tail sprang back at his face when it caught a snag among the bushes.

Coming to another lake, he decided to stop and eat his beaver and hung it on a branch. "I'll need a few sticks to roast it," he thought to himself and walked into the bush to fashion the roasting sticks. As he disappeared into the bush, Broadtail loosened himself from the branch and made for the lake.

While he was whittling the sticks in the bush, Wesakachak seemed to hear the slapping of a beavertail on water. When he finished whittling, he went back to the lake for his beaver. It was gone. And there in the middle of the lake, Broadtail did backward somersaults in the water. He did not look at the beaver so much. All he looked at was his tobacco pouch tied on the beaver's tail.

"Please, at least, give me back my tobacco pouch. I have my tinder, flint, tobacco and my most precious pipe in it," Wesakachak begged.

Broadtail did another somersault and disappeared into the water. Below, he gathered mud and applied it to the outside of the pouch.

"Here you are," Broadtail shouted as he flung the pouch by the string.

A tree stood by the water's edge and it caught to a branch. But at the same time, the mud on the pouch flew off and dropped in the water. Wesakachak was not watching too closely but as soon as he saw the splash of the mud, he thought it was his pouch. Going to the water's edge, he could make out his pouch in the water. Little did he realize it was a reflection of the pouch which was hanging just above his head. Wesakachak got down on all fours and started to probe the water's bottom with his hand. Finding nothing, he probed deeper. After a rest to wait for the disturbed muddy water to clear, he still saw his pouch at the bottom. This time he would probe deeper. Broadtail was having the time of his life laughing at Wesakachak's stupidity. When Wesakachak realized he was laughed at, his pride prompted him to probe still deeper. A loud splash and poor Wesakachak had slipped his grip. Only his legs showed above the water.

Only did he see his pouch as he crawled onto the bank, that again he started to stomp, howl and pull his hair in uncontrolled fury.

Jackson Beardy

PONTIAC'S WAR

Pontiac, war chief of the Ottawas, was furious! The French had been defeated by the English who now controlled the "west". Unlike the French the English gave no free ammunition and were in every way less friendly and less generous. Pontiac was determined to run the "red coats" out of the country.

He organized a war which became the fiercest opposition the English ever faced in North America. He led four tribes, inspired revolt in many more, captured nine forts, forced the abandonment of a tenth, and besieged two more.

A clever speaker as well as a wise general, he used the teachings of a very popular Delaware medicine man to gain the support he needed.

This Delaware, who was eager to make the acquaintance of the Master of Life, resolved to undertake a secret journey to his dwelling place in Paradise. But as he did not know how to reach that place, he waited for a dream to guide him. In his dream he was advised simply to set out and he would be guided along his route. Accordingly he equipped himself for a long journey and started. For eight days he travelled without discouragement, until he came to a clearing into which three trails converged. He did not know which one to take, but finally chose the widest. After following it for half a day, he encountered a great fire coming out of the earth. As it appeared to spread toward him he retraced his steps and took another trail. This, too, led him to a pit of fire, and he returned and started down the last path. He followed it to its end at the foot of a gleaming white mountain. Puzzled, he looked around and perceived a beautiful woman, clothed in white, who addressed him in his own tongue. She knew the purpose of his journey and advised him that his way lay across the mountain; but to ascend it he must first undress, bathe, and leave his clothes behind.

The Indian did as he was told, and when he had climbed to the top of the mountain he saw three villages ahead of him. He walked toward the most attractive one and was met at the gate by a man in white. This stranger greeted him and led him in to meet the Master of Life. The Divine Being took him by the hand and gave him a fancy hat which he was to sit on. Then the Master addressed him:

"I am the Master of Life, and since I know what you desire to know, and to whom you wish to speak, listen well to what I am going to say to you and to all the Indians:

"I am He who has created the heavens and the earth, the trees, lakes, rivers, all men, and all that you see and have seen upon the earth. Because I love you, you must do what I say and love, and not do what I hate. I do not love that you should drink to the point of madness, as you do; and I do not like that you should fight one another. You take two wives, or run after the wives of others; you do not well, and I hate that. You ought to have but one wife, and keep her till death. When you wish to go to war, you conjure and resort to the medicine dance, believing that you speak to me; you are mistaken, — it is to Manitou that you speak, an evil spirit who prompts you to nothing but wrong, and who listens to you out of ignorance of me.

"This land where you dwell I have made for you and not for others. Whence comes it that you permit the Whites upon your lands? Can you not live without them? I know that those whom you call the children of your Great Father supply your needs, but if you were not evil, as you are, you could surely do without them. You could live as you did live before knowing them, — before those whom you call your brothers had come upon your lands. Did you not live by the bow and arrow? You had no need of gun or powder, or anything else, and nevertheless you caught animals to live upon and to dress yourselves with their skins. But when I saw that you were given up to evil, I led the wild animals to the depths of the forest so that you had to depend upon your brothers to feed and shelter you. You have only to become good again and do what I wish, and I will send back the animals for your food. I do not forbid you to permit among you the children of your Father; I love them. They know me and pray to me, and I supply their wants and all they give you. But as to those who come to trouble your lands, — drive them out, make war upon them. I do not like them at all; they know me not, and are my enemies, and the enemies of your brothers. Send them back to the lands which I

The death of Pontiac.

have created for them and let them stay there. Here is a prayer which I give you in writing to learn by heart and to teach to the Indians and their children."

The Delaware confessed that he could not read, so the Master told him to give the prayer to his chief when he returned to his village. In summary the Master of Life repeated his injunctions:

"Do not drink more than once, or at most twice, in a day; have only one wife and do not run after the wives of others nor after the girls; do not fight among yourselves; do not "make medicine", but pray, because in "making medicine" one talks with the evil spirit; drive off your land those dogs clothed in red who will do you nothing but harm. And when you shall have need of anything address yourselves to me; and as to your brothers, I shall give to you as to them; do not sell to your brothers what I put on earth for food. In short, become good and you shall receive your needs. When you meet one another exchange greetings and proffer the left hand, which is nearest the heart. In all things I command you to repeat every morning and night the prayer which I have given you."

THE BATTLE-BIRDS

Mr. H. R. Schoolcraft was an explorer and American ethnologist. He recorded this battle song of the Ojibway over one hundred years ago.

THE BATTLE-BIRDS

The battle-birds swoop from the sky,
They thirst for the warrior's heart;
They look from their circles on high,
And scorn every flesh but the brave.

WILD HARVESTS

Ohiyesa, the Sioux, spent most of his childhood in Minnesota and Manitoba as a neighbour of the feared Ojibway. Although the eastern Sioux and the western Ojibway were bitter enemies they shared not only a similar country but similar customs such as collecting maple sap in the spring and wild rice in the fall. Ohiyesa remembered particularly the rice harvests in Minnesota, "Land of the Sky Blue Water", before war between the Sioux and the Americans forced his family to flee north to Manitoba.

The wild rice harvesters came in groups of fifteen to twenty families to a lake. The people, while they pitched their teepees upon the heights, if possible, for the sake of a good outlook, actually lived in their canoes upon the waters. The happiest of all, perhaps, were the young girls, who were all day long in their canoes, in twos and threes.

These girls learned to imitate the calls of the different water-fowls as a sort of signal to other members of the group. Even the old women and the boys adopted signals, so that while the population of

Frances Mike bends rice over the canoe with her left hand and knocks off the grains with three beats of her right. Her sticks keep a steady rhythm as she alternates from one side to the other.

the village was lost to sight in a thick field of wild rice, a meeting could be arranged without calling any one by his or her own name. It was a great convenience for those young men who sought an opportunity to meet certain girls, for there were many canoe paths through the rice.

August is the harvest month. There were many preliminary feasts of fish, ducks and venison, and offerings in honour of the "Water Chief", so that there might not be any drowning accident during the harvest. The preparation consisted of a series of feasts and offerings for many days, while women and men were making birch bark canoes, for nearly every member of the family must be provided with one for this occasion.

There were social events which enlivened the camp of the harvesters; such as feasts, dances and a canoe regatta, in which not only the men were participants, but women and young girls as well.

On the appointed day all the canoes were carried to the shore and placed upon the water with prayers and offerings. Each family took possession of the allotted field and tied all the grain in bundles of convenient size, allowing it to stand for a few days. Then they again entered the lake, assigning two persons to each canoe. One handled the paddle, while the foremost one gently drew the head of each bundle toward him and gave it a few strokes with a light rod. This caused the rice to fall into the bottom of the craft. The field was crossed in this manner back and forth until finished.

This was the easiest part of the harvest. The real work was when they prepared the rice for use. First of all, it must be made perfectly dry. They would spread it upon buffalo robes and mats, and sometimes upon layers of coarse swamp grass, and dry it in the sun. If the time was short, they would make a scaffold and spread upon it a certain thickness of the green grass and afterward the rice. Under this a fire was made, taking care that the grass did not catch fire.

When all the rice is gathered and dried, the hulling begins. A round hole is dug about two feet deep and the same in diameter. Then the rice is heated over a fire-place, and emptied into the hole while it is hot. A young man, having washed his feet and put on a new pair of moccasins, treads upon it until all is hulled. The women then put it upon a robe and begin to shake it so that the chaff will be separated by the wind.

During the hulling time there were prizes offered to the young men who could hull quickest and best. There were sometimes from twenty to fifty youths dancing with their feet in these holes.

Pretty moccasins were brought by shy girls to the men of their choice, asking them to hull rice. There were daily entertainments and the girls brought with them plenty of good things to eat.

Ohiyesa (Charles Eastman)

HUNGER STALKS THE HUNTERS

Kah-ge-gah-bowh, the son of a powerful medicine man, was born at Rice Lake. European missionaries visited his camp and in 1830 he was converted to Christianity. He was educated in such distant cities as Boston. As George Copway he became a Methodist missionary among the people of the Great Lakes. In his autobiography he describes the rough but exciting days of his childhood.

Once we left Rice Lake in the fall, and went up the river in canoes, above Bellmont Lake. There were five families about to hunt with my father, on his grounds. The winter began, and the river having frozen over, we left the canoes, the dried venison, the beaver, and some flour and pork; and when we had gone further north, say about sixty miles from the whites, for the purpose of hunting, the snow fell for five days in succession to such a depth, that it was impossible to shoot or trap anything. Our provisions were exhausted, and we had no means to get any more. Here we were. The snow about five feet deep; our wigwam buried; the branches of the trees falling around us, and cracking from the weight of the snow.

Our mother boiled birch bark for my sister and myself that we might not starve. On the seventh day some of them were so weak that they could not raise themselves, and others could not stand alone. They could only crawl in and out of the wigwam. We parched beaver skins and old moccasins for food. On the ninth day none of the men were able to go abroad, except my father and uncle. On the tenth day, still being without food, those only who were able to walk about the wigwam, were my father, my grandmother, my sister, and myself. O how distressing to see the starving Indians lying about the wigwam with hungry and eager looks; the children would cry for something to eat. My poor mother would heave *bitter sighs of despair,* the tears falling from her cheeks as she kissed us. Wood, though plenty, could not be obtained, on account of the feebleness of our limbs.

My father, at times, would draw near the fire, and rehearse some prayer to the gods. It appeared to him that there was no way of escape; the men, women and children dying; some of them were speechless. The wigwam was cold and dark, and covered with snow. On the eleventh day, just before daylight, my father fell into a sleep; he soon awoke and said to me, "My son, the Great Spirit is about to bless us; this night in my dream I saw a person coming from the east, walking on the tops of the trees. He told me that we should obtain two beavers this morning about nine o'clock. Put on your moccasins and go along with me to the river, and we will hunt the beaver, perhaps for the last time." I saw that his countenance beamed with delight; he was full of confidence. I put on my moccasins and carried my snow shoes, staggering along behind him, about half a mile. Having made a fire near the river, where there was an air hole, through which the beaver had come up during the night, my father tied a gun to a stump, with the muzzle towards the air hole; he also tied a string to the trigger, and said "should you see the beaver rise, pull the string and you will kill it." I stood by the fire with the string in my hand. I soon heard a noise occasioned by the blow of his tomahawk; he had killed a beaver, and he brought it to me. As he laid it down, he said "then the Great Spirit will not let us die here;" adding, as before, "if you see the beaver, rise, and pull the string." He left me, I soon saw the nose of one; but I did not shoot. Presently another came up; I pulled the trigger, and off the gun went. I could not see for some time for the smoke. My father ran towards me, took the two beavers and laid them side by side; then pointing to the sun, said, "Do you see the sun; The Great Spirit informed me that we should kill these two about this time this morning. We will yet see our relatives at Rice Lake; now let us go home and see if they are still alive."

George Copway

Virginia and Gladys by Daphne (Odjig) Beavon

THE SKY CLEARS

The grand medicine society of the Ojibway is called the Midéwi-win. The men and women who are members of the society have great healing powers. In times past, they often remembered their Midé songs by painting sketches on birch bark.

THE SKY CLEARS

Verily
The sky clears
When my Midé drum
Sounds
For me.
Verily
The waters are smooth
When my Midé drum
Sounds
For me.

MY PEOPLE THE GREAT OJIBWAY

Norval Morriseau is one of the most famous of Canada's artists. His paintings are owned by art lovers across Canada and his huge mural covered one entire side of the Indians of Canada Pavilion at Expo 67 in Montreal.

His paintings, which always present the Ojibway point of view, have prompted many questions and in 1965 he wrote a book about the Ojibway in which he explained some of his beliefs.

Mr. Morriseau is a practising Christian and according to some Ojibway people he has combined Christian ideas with those of the Ojibway.

The great Ojibway people of North America believed there was one God, Gitchi Manitou, who was their only God and whom they worshipped. The Ojibway believed that there were six layers of heaven. One to four were reserved for all the respected tribes of the Indian people, the fifth heaven was reserved for people who had white skins and the sixth layer was for the Great Spirit and his company alone. The Ojibway had medicine dreams about all these layers except the sixth layer. No mind could penetrate to this place that was reserved for the Great Spirit. In all the four layers there were Ojibway or Indian guardians who wore scarlet clothing with pointed hoods like caps, Heaven People to guard these heavens set aside for all Indian people.

Each Indian went to one of these layers according to the way he behaved himself on earth. Everyone went to heaven no matter what he did; after all there was lots of room on the four layers. God is good and there was no such belief as hell. We do not believe there could be such a place. God, the giver of life, is all-good in every way and we cannot believe he would make the place called hell by our White brothers. Also although it is said from time to time in history that we were all a bunch of savages and needed the salvation of God very badly, I believe the Ojibway had the best belief about heaven. Where those of white origin went if they did wrong I cannot say. After all, my book concerns only Indian people, especially the Ojibway.

I myself, living in this modern era, believe no one knows where heaven is, but my people, the great Ojibway, often tried to find out. I have given you some idea of our beliefs. Even if these do not all sound convincing, at least I can say we had good imaginations.

People say that heaven is up in the great skies beyond the stars. If a rocket ship left the earth today, I understand it would travel for a long time and still not reach anywhere, for space is vast. As for those of my people who claimed to have gone some place after they were dead and then came back in a matter of two to three days, my idea is, where could they have gone? If the rocket ship could travel for ever without finding heaven, then there must be a heaven right here on earth that we pass every day without being able to penetrate its invisible wall. When a human body dies, however, and the soul leaves the body, then the soul itself can pass through this wall that we cannot pass in our human bodies.

Let me explain. We pass this wall every day. We never bump against it, but still it is there. Our human body could never go into what is on the other side of that wall, but a soul could penetrate it. If a soul that left this earth and penetrated the wall looked back, it would see a different place. But there would still be a wall in heaven, too, and it could be the earth on the other side.

So this I believe is the way a person goes after he is dead. If there is no wall, though, there must be a lot of souls travelling yet that have never reached their destination, unless the soul itself travels faster than a rocket ship.

Norval Morriseau

NO LONGER THE MIDDLE FIVE

A hundred years ago Indian boys in eastern Canada and the United States were sent to boarding schools. When Francis La Flesche, an

Omaha, first entered school he was terrified by Grey-beard — the principal — and by all the other strange things. It was there that he met Brush, the orphan boy, who helped him and who soon became his friend and hero. Brush was unofficial leader of the gang of five boys who were not the oldest and not the youngest. They were the "Middle Five".

The clock struck the hour of twelve; I sat up listening. There was a stir and the sound of a voice that startled me. It was only Warren moving and talking in his sleep. I went stealthily to the head of the stairs, then listened again. I could only hear the throbbing of my heart, and the rasping pulsations in my ears. After a pause which seemed interminable, I put one foot down the first step, the board sprang under my weight, and creaked. Again I paused to listen; there was no stir, and I went on. Every little sound in the stillness of the night seemed exaggerated, and I was often startled, but I went on and reached the door of Brush's room. I scratched the panel three times. There was a movement within, and a slight cough. Slowly I turned the knob and opened the door. I entered, closed the door, but left it unlatched.

A candle stood burning in the midst of a number of bottles on a little table near the head of the bed. I knelt by the bedside, and Brush put his arm around my neck. We were silent for a while, finally he whispered in the Omaha tongue:

"I'm glad you came; I've been wanting to talk to you. They tell me I am better; but I know I am dying."

Oppressed with ominous dread, I cried out, interrupting him, "Don't say that! Oh, don't say that!"

But he went on, "You mustn't be troubled; I'm all right; I'm not afraid; I know God will take care of me. I have wanted to stay with you boys, but I can't. You've all been good to me. My strength is going, I must hurry, — tell the boys I want them to learn; I know you will, but the other boys don't care. I want them to learn, and to think. You'll tell them, won't you?"

He slipped his hand under the pillow, brought out his broken-bladed jacknife, and put it in my hand, then said, "I wish I had something to give to each one of the boys before I go. I have nothing in the world but this knife. I love all of you; but you understand me, so I give it to you. That's all. Let me rest a little, then you must go."

After a moment's stillness the door opened very gently, and the floor near it creaked as though there were footsteps. A breath of wind came and moved the flickering flame of the candle round and round. The boy stared fixedly through the vacant doorway. There was something strange and unnatural in his look as, with one arm still around me, he stretched the other toward the door, and, in a loud whisper, said, "My grandfather! He calls me. I'm coming, I'm coming!"

There was a sound of a movement around the room; Brush's eyes followed it until they again rested upon the open door, which swung to with a soft click; then he closed his eyes.

I crept closer to the sick boy; I was quivering with fear.

Brush opened his eyes again, he had felt me trembling. "Are you cold?" he asked.

Just then I heard footsteps in the girls' play-room; this time they were real; Brush heard them too.

"Superintendent," he said with an effort.

When I crept into my bed the clock below struck one. For a long while I lay awake. I could hear noises downstairs, Grey-beard's door open and close, and the door of Brush's room. I heard a window raised, then everything became still.

We did not know how fondly we were attached to Brush, how truly he had been our leader, until we four, left alone, lingered around his grave in the shadowy darkness of night, each one reluctant to leave.

The Mission bell rang for evening service, and with slow steps we moved toward the school — no longer "The Middle Five".

Francis La Flesche

LOVE SONGS

Among the Ojibway, love songs were sometimes used as part of a love spell and their power was something to fear. The following songs are more concerned with sorrow or hope, the type often accompanied by a flute, drum, or rattle.

"I Will Walk" is a very old courting song. The young man walked slowly through the camp singing each verse several times so that his girl would have plenty of time to make up her mind to welcome him.

A Loon I Thought It Was

A loon I thought it was
But it was my love's splashing oar,
To Sault Ste. Marie he has departed
My love has gone on before me
Never again can I see him
A loon I thought it was
But it was my love's splashing oar.

Love Song

Oh
I am thinking
Oh
I am thinking
I have found my lover
Oh
I think it is so!

I Will Walk

I will walk into somebody's dwelling
Into somebody's dwelling will I walk

To thy dwelling, my dearly beloved
Some night will I walk will I walk

Some night in the winter, my beloved
To thy dwelling will I walk, will I walk

This very night, my beloved
To thy dwelling will I walk will I walk.

CRASHING THUNDER HAS A FIGHT

Among the Winnebago all strong men obtain a vision. Crashing Thunder was unsuccessful in spite of his father's teachings. Not wishing to disappoint his family he pretended that he had obtained a guardian spirit. His life became one pretence after another and his world was filled with violence.

We had to spend sixty days in jail. During my imprisonment I never had my hair cut and from that time on, I always wore it long. I told the people that a spirit called *Foolish-one* had instructed me to do this and that he had blessed me. I also told my older brother, the one who was still living, to do the same thing and that if he, too, let his hair grow, *Foolish-one* would bless him with long life. From that time on I wore long hair.

After that I joined a show of the Whites. People liked me very much on account of my long hair and I was well paid. I kept on drinking all the time. I there learned to ride a bicycle and mount and ride wild horses. I used to call myself a cowboy, principally because I wore my hair long. Many vicious horses did I ride, and I was thrown off many times. I did all this not because I felt myself to be an expert, but because I was wild. On one occasion I took part in a bicycle ride on a regular racetrack. I was in full Indian costume and wore long hair.

The show I had joined played at St. Paul. I took part in it every summer. I became acquainted with many people and so I was asked to come again every year. Finally it got so that I would not even return to the Indians in winter.

Once we were to give our show at a certain place for the last time, for the cold weather was setting in. It was thus our last day. One of the boys came to me and told me that someone had struck him. I got angry and told him to point out the person who had done it. After the show was finished we put on our civilian clothes and took our hand-bags. "None of you must go out alone," I warned them, "for you might get hurt." One of my boys was on horseback and was taking his horse to water it at a trough. His pony was taken away from him and he returned without it. His hat, too, had been stolen. Indeed he barely escaped with his life. "Come, let us go back," I said. I told the other boys to go right on and not to worry about me. I gave them my handbag and then returned to the place where the first boy had been attacked. Before we got there the same boy was attacked and set upon with clubs. We were right in the midst of a big crowd of Whites. These shouted and chased him. When they saw me they started for me. I fought them with my bare fists, turning from side to side. I was completely surrounded by them. Whenever any one got near enough to me I struck him. Then I started to run and was hit on the head, but I was not knocked unconscious. I was now angry and I struck out at all within reach. If I had had a weapon I would have killed some of them. Several now fell upon me and I was struck on the head until it was entirely covered with blood. I started for the show tents which had not yet been taken down. Just then the man who had begun all the trouble came toward me with a hatchet. I went for him and when he raised the hatchet I struck him and knocked him down, for I hit him straight in the mouth.

A policeman now came forward and led me to our show tents. I was covered with blood. The women were weeping and told the policeman who I was, that it was not my fault and that I had not been drinking. I was taken to jail. I told the policeman that we ought not to be locked up for we had not started the trouble. The others ought to be locked up, we said, for it was the particular man who had hit my boy who had been drinking.

"You are right," said the policeman. "I will go back and look for your things. Yet you ought not to be on the street for you have hurt many people. You had better stay in jail for a few hours for many people are on the watch for you. Now I'll go for your pony and then you can do what you like." They put me in jail and there I found the Indian about whom all the trouble had started. "Well, this is good," he said. "I thought they had killed you. Well, how many did you kill?" "I didn't kill any one," I answered. "It is good, for I thought they had either killed you or that you had killed them."

Then I washed the blood from my head soon after the policeman returned and brought my pony with him, as well as my hat. Then he said, "You are to go home immediately. It is true that you have been dealt with unfairly, but this is a regular fair town, and if any trouble starts in the courts about this affair, it will hurt our fairs in the future. We shall therefore not go to law about it. The man who started the trouble is the owner of a large hotel, and in addition, owns a trotting horse. You have knocked out all the teeth of this hotel-keeper, and we do not know whether he will live or not. You have bruised other people, too badly. So you had better go home."

As told to Paul Radin

I AM CONVERTED

Crashing Thunder's family had taken up the Peyote religion. He did not want to join them because he had heard that the Peyote people were bad people. He knew that they ate the peyote bud from the mescal cactus and that the bud contained a drug which helped produce visions. He decided to try the peyote bud so that he too could find the new religion that had come out of the west. Perhaps he would find the long-sought vision.

When we arrived at the meeting, the leader asked me to sit near him and there I was placed. He urged me to eat many peyote and I did so. Now the leaders of the ceremony always place the sacred objects in front of themselves. The sacred peyote was also placed there. Now the one this particular leader placed in front of himself this time was a very small one. "Why does he have a very small one?" I thought to myself. However, I did not think of this matter long.

It was now late at night. I had eaten a lot of peyote and felt rather tired. I suffered considerably. After a while I looked at the peyote, and there I saw an eagle standing with outspread wings. It was as beautiful a sight as could well be observed. Each of the feathers seemed to have a mark. The eagle stood there looking at me. I turned my gaze thinking that perhaps there was something the matter with my sight, but then when I looked again the eagle was still present. Again I turned around and when I looked at the spot where the eagle stood, it was gone and only the small peyote remained. I then watched the other people, but they all had their heads bowed and were praying.

Suddenly I saw a lion lying in the same place where before I had seen the eagle. I watched it very closely and when I turned my eyes for the least little bit, it disappeared. "I suppose all those present are aware of this and I am just beginning to find out," I thought. Then I saw a small person at the same place. He wore blue clothes and a shining brimmed cap. He had on a soldier's uniform and was sitting on the arm of the person who was drumming, scrutinizing everybody. He was a little man but perfect in all proportions. Finally I lost sight of him. I was very much surprised indeed. I sat very quietly. "So this is what it is," I thought. "This is what they all probably see and which I am just now beginning to find out."

Then I prayed to Earthmaker, to God:

"This, your ceremony, let me hereafter perform!"

Before I joined the Peyote I went about in a most pitiable condition, and now I am living happily and my wife has a fine baby.

As told to Paul Radin

Chapter VIII

The Great Tree of Peace

The Tree is the law. Its branches offer protection. The white roots stretch to the ends of the earth and anyone taking hold of the white root and tracing it to its source will find Peace.

Dekanawidah, the Founder, had a vision of universal peace. With Hiawatha as his speaker he journeyed throughout Iroquoia persuading the people and the chiefs to join the League. He persuaded the Mohawk, Oneida, Cayuga, and Seneca but Atotaho, the evil wizard of the Onondaga, refused to hear the gai-weiio (good word); Dekanawidah's convictions triumphed and when Atotaho accepted the White Roots of Peace the League was formed. The first grand meeting of the "Lords of the Confederacy" took place on Onondaga Lake before the year 1450.

The League of the Long House was designed to welcome all men in peace and the members of the Five Nations did everything they could to live up to that ideal. The Tuscaroras were admitted to almost full membership and peoples such as the English and the Ojibway were granted alliances that stood for centuries. Even during war—an activity at which they excelled to such an extent that they terrified their neighbours—they granted complete forgiveness to their enemies. Thousands of prisoners were adopted into the tribe as free and equal members.

Their alliance with the British during the American Revolution brought their golden age of dominance to an end. Persuaded by the

Mohawk chief, Joseph Brant, many of the people dropped their neutrality to fight and lose with the British. At the end of that war they fled with other Loyalists to Canada where the Lords rekindled their council fires.

It was at this time the Seneca prophet Handsome Lake revived and strengthened the ancient Long House religion, the religion which enlightens the hearts and minds of thousands of Iroquois today.

The need for an understanding of Dekanawidah's dream of Peace is greater today than it ever was.

THE WORLD ON THE TURTLE'S BACK

John Dockstader, Hia-yon-os, sculptor, artist, author, and businessman, grew up on the Six Nations reserve where he and his friends heard about the beginning of the world from the old people sitting around the kitchen stove during long happy evenings.

Not all the children grew up to become story tellers but John had an advantage. His great-grandfather John Arthur Gibson, a Seneca chief, was a famous orator and one of the first Iroquois to record and preserve the legends and stories of his people. His grandfather Simeon Gibson was no less famous as a story teller.

In ancient times there dwelled in the Sky-world a great and powerful chief, "He The Sky Holder". In this Sky-world there was neither light nor darkness. Near the lodge of this great chief grew the Great Tree of Light. The blossoms from this tree lighted the Sky-world. The Beings that lived in this world possessed great wisdom and lived in peace.

The chief took a young wife named Mature Flowers, but did not find happiness because the Fire-Dragon of jealousy filled his mind. "He The Sky Holder" uprooted the Great Tree of Light and invited his wife to sit beside him and look down on the world below. While she was doing this he crept behind her and gave her a mighty shove. As she fell she grasped at the roots of the Tree of Light and the earth but she could not save herself from falling through the hole in the sky.

The world below was populated with man-creatures of the sea and of the air for there was only water. These creatures seeing the Sky-woman falling toward them held a council and decided that she should be saved since she had the power to create.

The creatures of the air flew up to bring her gently down on their wings. The water creatures volunteered to dive to the bottom of the sea and bring up some mud so that she might have a safe place on which to rest. Many tried but all failed and some were drowned.

Finally Muskrat tried and after a long time had passed he rose to the surface but he too had drowned. In his lifeless paws and mouth he held some of the precious mud from the bottom of the sea.

Beaver tried to hold the mud on his back but it became too heavy and he asked that someone else take on the burden. Turtle tried next and Beaver placed the mud upon his back. The creatures of the air then placed Sky-woman upon this island on the Turtle's back and it immediately began to grow. As she walked about, the seeds from her clothing fell to the earth and in her footsteps vegetation sprang up instantly.

Just as the world grew to a suitable size Sky-woman gave birth to a woman child. This child soon grew to maidenhood and had many suitors among the Beings that lived in this world. These beings had the power to transform themselves into human form at will. The maiden, after asking her mother's advice, rejected all these proposals but accepted the Being in scalloped leggings and robe.

She soon gave birth to twin male beings but died because of the evil nature of the younger child. She was buried and from her grave grew the Three Sisters, Squash, Corn, and Beans. She then became known as Earth-Mother.

Sky-woman, now a grandmother, named the Eldest Brother, who was good minded, "He Grasps The Sky With Both Hands". The Younger Brother, who had purposely caused the death of his mother, was evil and ugly to look upon and was named "Flint".

"He Grasps The Sky With Both Hands" sought out his father and finding him asked for wisdom and power to create the good things for this earth. He then created plants, animals, and songbirds. When all this was completed he created man after himself and called him "Sapling", then he created woman and called her "Growing Flower". In the sky he placed Our Grandmother the Moon, Elder Brother the Sun, Day Bringer the Morning Star, and the path to the Sky-world the Milky Way and gave them all duties to perform.

His evil brother "Flint" tried to imitate his works but only succeeded in creating thistles, thorns, bats, monsters, and serpents. Rivers had currents that ran both ways for ease of travel till "Flint" made falls and rapids. He stunted the growth of food and caused winter to be invented. All of his creations were of no use to man. He finally challenged his brother to a duel to determine who should control man. "Flint" was defeated and was banished forever.

"Good-Minded" returned to the Sky-world but returned to earth four times to teach the people, whose bodies he created, the use of plants and animals and the four ceremonies of Thanksgiving. He taught them to live in peace and harmony and to seek out human values. When all his work was completed he left for the Sky-world promising to return when the rains came from the East, saying, "Thus shall it continue to be in the future that there shall be always two tribes of people living on either side of the river."

John Dockstader

THE CORN HUSKER

In the old days all the land around the Iroquois village was cleared. Corn, beans, and squash were planted together and were so important in the lives of the people that they were called the Three Sisters.

In this poem E. Pauline Johnson, the famous Mohawk poetess, thinks back to those other days.

THE CORN HUSKER

Hard by the Indian lodges, where the bush
   Breaks in a clearing, through ill-fashioned fields,
She comes to labour, when the first still hush
   Of autumn follows large and recent yields.

Age in her fingers, hunger in her face,
   Her shoulders stooped with weight of work and years,
But rich in tawny colouring of her race,
   She comes a-field to strip the purple ears.

And all her thoughts are with the days gone by,
   Ere might's injustice banished from their lands
Her people, that to-day unheeded lie,
   Like the dead husks that rustle through her hands.

E. Pauline Johnson

THAYENDANEGA

Thayendanega, a Mohawk who was also known as Joseph Brant, may be one of the most controversial men in Iroquois history. He was a devout Anglican and a brother-in-law of Sir William Johnson who was the King of England's "Sole Agent for all Affairs to the Six Nations and other Northern Indians". During the American War of Independence Joseph not only decided to side with the British but also persuaded other Iroquois to take an active part in the war. This decision made him a hero to some but a villain to others.

Mrs. Ethel Brant Monture has written a biography of her famous Mohawk ancestor from which the following anecdotes are taken.

Joseph and the rest of the Mohawks came to the conclusion that they must know whether the British would or would not help them recover their lands. Since no one at Montreal would tell them, Sir Guy Carleton arranged for Joseph to go to England with John Deseronto, his cousin.

Lord Jeffrey Amherst, who had been commander-in-chief of the British forces in America, gave a great dinner in Joseph's honour. In his toast Amherst referred to Joseph as "His Majesty's greatest American subject". Charles James Fox, the statesman and orator, was asked to speak, but he begged Joseph to respond for himself. Joseph was reluctant, saying, "His Majesty has a good many great American subjects — some of whom," he added with a flash of a smile, "are greater than they are good!"

* * *

Joseph attended a theatre party at the Drury Lane Theatre to witness a performance of *Romeo and Juliet*. The Lady Ossory, a member of a famous Irish family, watched Joseph with amusement and asked him, "What do you think of that kind of love-making, Captain Brant?" Joseph retorted, "There is too much of it, your ladyship." "Why do you say that?" said the lady, and Joseph answered quickly, "Because your ladyship, no lover worth a lady's while would waste his time and breath in all that speech-making. If my people were to make love that way our race would be extinct in two generations."

* * *

As parting gifts an old friend, Thomas Pownall, gave Deseronto and Joseph each a London rifle.

They returned on the ship the *Harriott*. The vessel was at sea for six weeks, taking a southern route in order to avoid Yankee privateers. One sunny morning Joseph and Deseronto were lying on the deck when they heard the lookout shouting to the captain, who also began to shout orders. As they watched, sail after sail was shaken out, and the masts bent under the push of the wind. The captain yelled, "Privateer!" as a hawk-winged vessel with a sharp hull grew large on the horizon. The *Harriott* heeled and righted herself painfully. In the stern two small cannons popped and fell short but solid shot from the raider ripped holes in the *Harriott's* canvas.

Speaking in Mohawk, Joseph and Deseronto agreed to try out their new rifles. The privateer was near enough to bring her crewmen into view. Joseph knelt to rest his rifle on the rail and Deseronto acted as lookout, telling Joseph to aim for the tall captain directing the gunfire. As he came in range Joseph squeezed the trigger and the captain fell from view. Deseronto gave Joseph his gun and said a man in a blue cap was giving orders. Joseph knelt waiting for the *Harriott* to lift on a wave, and with his next shot the blue hat was gone. Deseronto supplied Joseph with loaded rifles and he and Deseronto picked off five men from the raider. Shells from the privateer had shattered the mast and those on the *Harriott* were all gashed with spinters and peppered with grape shot. The sailors were screaming, but the captain cursed and bawled at them to climb up and cut away the shattered rigging. Blood ran down Joseph's face and Deseronto was holding his arm. The raider turned away and the *Harriott* limped into New York with ragged sail. To the privateers the incident meant chiefly a regrettable piece of lost booty; to the Mohawks it was a good opportunity to test a hunter's London rifle.

* * *

THE GREAT TREE OF PEACE   153

He had many worries concerning the Indians in general and concerning himself personally. One special grief had been with him for many years; that was his son Isaac, beloved as his first-born son but unresponsive and difficult to guide. In the time of the American Revolution he had been unable to keep Isaac near him and was often forced to leave him to fend for himself and he thought this was the reason that Isaac grew away from him. He could never win Isaac's confidence, although he never stopped trying. Isaac had gone for a time to school in Philadelphia, and he went with delegations to other tribes many times, sometimes with much credit, for he was fine-looking and could be very agreeable. His father had moments of great pride in him but Isaac brought him his deepest grief.

Isaac lived in his father's house where he was given every opportunity and shown every courtesy; but he was resentful of his father in every way. He was jealous of his father and his father's prestige, and jealous of Catherine [Joseph's second wife] and her children. Drinking rum put Isaac into completely unmanageable moods. Once in a drunken fight he killed a white saddlemaker who was a deserter from General Wayne's American army.

A bitter finish was made finally in a tavern which was also a supply depot. Isaac and some companions were drinking and arguing there and Joseph, who was in an adjoining room transacting business, heard the noise and recognized Isaac's voice. He went in to quiet him, but Isaac in a rage attacked him with a knife and Joseph had to defend himself. In the fight that followed, Isaac was wounded. He refused to have the wound cared for and the infection that set in killed him. Joseph gave himself up and the Canadian court acquitted him. But sorrow almost killed him; he resigned from all his activities and gave himself up to despondency. His People of the Longhouse stood beside him in his trouble; they held a council and deliberated on all the facts. Then they sent Joseph a letter, for he had shut himself away from them: "Brother, we have considered your case. We sympathize with you. You are bereaved of a beloved son. But that son raised his hand against the kindest of fathers. His death was caused by his own hand. With one voice we take away all blame from you. We tender you condolence. May the Great Spirit give you consolation and comfort under your affliction." The kindness of the Council was the spur Joseph needed to bring him out of his despair.

Ethel B. Monture

THE HIDEOUS ONE

The power to heal, cure, and protect others is a gift. It is granted only to those who are able to prepare themselves spiritually through prayers and fasting. One of the most important medicine societies is the False Face Society and of all the protectors "Old Broken Nose" is the most important. Lorna Jamieson Thomas of the Six Nations reserve tells how it all began.

The Creator was treading the paths of earth looking over the results of His efforts. He met a manlike creature with a very hideous face and long straggly hair. This creature had human structure but was terribly hideous and the long straggly hair made quite a sight. With a huge nose set between two huge eyes and an immense mouth, he carried a rattle made from the shell of a snapping turtle and also a long staff.

Upon their encounter both of them asked similar questions: "For what purpose do you tread upon this land?"

An Iroquois wearing a broken-nose mask.

They both had the same answer: "I am reviewing the works of my efforts."

Well now, here we find two beings with similar ideas and surely there can only be one being responsible for this great splendour and so the dispute had to be settled.

The Great Spirit then spoke again saying: "We must now make a test to see who is responsible for creating the earth and all its splendour. Come now and we shall approach yonder mountain. See, next to the mountain stands a great rock. We must now test to see which of us can make that rock move without touching it."

This agreed, the pair moved to a suitable spot where it was decided that the hideous one be the first to test his ability. He then began making a great racket by rubbing his great huge rattle upon the great staff that he carried and at the same time making great loud throaty sounds that went somewhat like, "Yon'h hon'h-Hon'h!"

The great rock began to tremble and finally it began to move back and forth. The hideous one began to make a greater racket than ever but after such exhausting effort he could do no more than to make the great rock sway back and forth. He then turned to the Great Spirit and announced that it was now up to Him to try His efforts at the test.

The Great Spirit nodded and asked the ugly one to turn his back to the rock. The ugly one agreed and did as the Creator asked. The Creator then took a slender whip from a nearby clump of young hickory saplings. He waved the whip toward the rock and through His great mind ran these thoughts, "Would thou yonder rock come forth to me."

The rock once again began to tremble and then it started to move toward the pair of figures making the test of strength. It finally stopped only inches away from the pair and it was then that the Great Spirit told the ugly one that he may now turn around to look upon the results of the Creator's effort.

The hideous one turned quickly and the rock was so close behind him that he accidently bumped his enormous nose upon the face of the rock and flattened it slightly to one side of his face. That is the reason that to this day the great masks are made with the huge nose slightly flattened to one side of the face. It was agreed then that the more powerful of the pair was indeed the Great Spirit and was therefore the Creator of all things. So now the ugly creature turned once more to the Great Spirit saying: "Almighty one, with your kind permission I greatly desire to remain upon the face of the earth to henceforth be known as the 'grandfather' of Your children. I will help them in future whenever I am able. With my hideous face I shall have no trouble driving away many of the evils which might otherwise harm them. I will frighten away the evils in the springtime and help to cleanse the earth when You send forth the fresh growths of each new season. I promise to remain in the depths of the great forests so that I will not frighten the people but I will always be near enough at hand to be of help if I am needed even to the extent of medicinal purposes so that they may always be blessed with the gift of good health so long as You so desire."

Lorna Jamieson Thomas

SAGAYEWATHA SPEAKS

Sagayewatha (He Keeps Them Awake), the Seneca chief whom the English called Red Jacket, was born in 1750 and learned early that truth was a powerful but dangerous weapon. People do not like to hear unpleasant truths.

He was known far and wide as a persuasive orator. He spoke against war and warned his people against the greed of white land speculators. He was particularly wary of the missionary and of Christianity and he expressed his feelings eloquently in reply to a missionary who, in 1805, had come to Buffalo, New York, to Christianize the Iroquois.

Brother, you say you want an answer to your talk before you leave this place. It is right you should have one, as you are a great distance from home, and we do not wish to detain you; but we will first look back a little, and tell you what our fathers have told us, and what we have heard from the white people.

Brother, listen to what we say. There was a time when our forefathers owned this great island. Their seats extended from the rising to the setting sun. The Great Spirit had made it for the use of the Indians. He had created the buffalo, the deer, and other animals for food. He made the bear and the beaver, and their skins served us for clothing. He had scattered them over the country, and taught us how to take them. He had caused the earth to produce corn for bread. All this he had done for his red children because he loved them. If we had any disputes about hunting grounds, they were generally settled without the shedding of much blood: but an evil day came upon us; your forefathers crossed the great waters and landed on this island. Their numbers were small; they found friends, not enemies; they told us they had fled from their own country for fear of wicked men, and come here to enjoy their religion. They asked for a small seat; we took pity on them, granted their request, and they sat down among us; we gave them corn and meat; they gave us poison in return. The white people had now found our country, tidings were carried back, and more came among us; yet we did not fear them, we took them to be friends; they called us brothers; we believed them and gave them a larger seat. At length their number had greatly increased; they wanted more land; they wanted our country. Our eyes were opened, and our minds became uneasy. Wars took place; Indians were hired to fight against Indians, and many of our people were destroyed. They also brought strong liquors among us: it was strong and powerful, and has slain thousands.

Brother, our seats were once large, and yours were very small; you have now become a great people, and we have scarcely left a place to spread our blankets; you have got our country, but are not satisfied; you want to force your religion upon us.

Brother, we are told that your religion was given to your fore-fathers, and has been handed down from father to son. We also have a religion which was given to our forefathers, and has been handed down to us their children. We worship that way. It teaches us to be thankful for all the favours we receive; to love each other, and to be united. We never quarrel about religion.

Brother, the Great Spirit has made us all; but he has made a great difference between his white and red children; he has given us a different complexion, and different customs; to you he has given the arts; to these he has not opened our eyes; we know these things to be true. Since he has made so great a difference between us in other

Sagayewatha.

things, why may we not conclude that he has given us a different religion according to our understanding; the Great Spirit does right; he knows what is best for his children; we are satisfied.

Brother, we are told that you have been preaching to white people in this place; these people are our neighbours, we are acquainted with them; we will wait a little while and see what effect your preaching has upon them. If we find it does them good, makes them honest, and less disposed to cheat Indians, we will then consider again what you have said.

Sagayewatha

OJISTOH

E. Pauline Johnson (Tekahionwake) was born on the Six Nations reserve at Chiefswood, her father's estate. Her father was Onwanonsyshon (G. H. M. Johnson) a chief of the Mohawk tribe. Her mother was an English woman.

She was able to blend her Mohawk and English heritage and to select the best from both, but her first love was her father's people.

OJISTOH

I am Ojistoh, I am she, the wife
Of him whose name breathes bravery and life
And courage to the tribe that calls him chief.
I am Ojistoh, his white star, and he
Is land, and lake, and sky — and soul to me.

Ah! but they hated him, those Huron braves,
Him who had flung their warriors into graves,
Him who had crushed them underneath his heel
Whose arm was iron, and whose heart was steel
To all — save me, Ojistoh, chosen wife
Of my great Mohawk, white star of his life.

Ah! but they hated him, and councilled long
With subtle witchcraft how to work him wrong;
How to avenge their dead, and strike him where
His pride was highest, and his fame most fair.
Their hearts grew weak as women at his name:
They dared no war-path since my Mohawk came
With ashen bow, and flinten arrow-head
To pierce their craven bodies; but their dead
Must be avenged. Avenged? They dared not walk
In day and meet his deadly tomahawk;
They dared not face his fearless scalping knife;
So — Niyoh! — then they thought of me, his wife.

O! evil, evil face of them they sent
With evil Huron speech: "Would I consent
To take of wealth? be queen of all their tribe?
Have wampum ermine?" Back I flung the bribe
Into their teeth, and said, "While I have life
Know this — Ojistoh is the Mohawk's wife."

Wah! how we struggled! But their arms were strong.
They flung me on their pony's back, with thong

Round ankle, wrist, and shoulder. Then upleapt
The one I hated most: his eye he swept
Over my misery, and sneering said,
"Thus, fair Ojistoh, we avenge our dead."

And we two rode, rode as a sea wind-chased,
I, bound with buckskin to his hated waist,
He, sneering, laughing, jeering, while he lashed
The horse to foam, as on and on we dashed.
Plunging through creek and river, bush and trail,
On, on we galloped like a northern gale.
At last, his distant Huron fires aflame
We saw, and nearer, nearer still we came.

I, bound behind him in the captive's place,
Scarcely could see the outline of his face.
I smiled, and laid my cheek against his back;
"Loose thou my hands," I said. "This pace let slack.
Forget we now that thou and I are foes.
I like thee well, and wish to clasp thee close;
I like the courage of thine eye and brow;
I like thee better than my Mohawk now."

He cut the cords; we ceased our maddened haste
I wound my arms about his tawny waist;
My hand crept up the buckskin of his belt;
His knife hilt in my burning palm I felt;
One hand caressed his cheek, the other drew
The weapon softly — "I love you, love you,"
I whispered, "love you as my life."
And — buried in his back his scalping knife.

Ha! how I rode, as a sea wind-chased,
Mad with sudden freedom, made with haste,
Back to my Mohawk and my home. I lashed
That horse to foam, as on and on I dashed.
Plunging thro' creek and river, bush and trail,

On, on I galloped like a northern gale.
And then my distant Mohawk's fires aflame
I saw, as nearer, near still I came,
My hands all wet, stained with a life's red dye,
But pure my soul, pure as those stars on high —
"My Mohawk's pure white star, Ojistoh, still am I."

E. Pauline Johnson

HANDSOME LAKE

The Seneca along with Brant and the English had been defeated by the American rebels and were depressed and disorganized. The constant influx of more and more settlers and the steady flow of liquor combined to destroy many. Handsome Lake was one of those who couldn't resist whiskey.

At his lowest ebb Handsome Lake had a vision which formed the basis of the new Long House religion. This story of his inspiration is told by the late Arthur C. Parker, himself a Seneca and a noted anthropologist, in his book, Red Jacket: Last of the Seneca.

In a small shack near Burnt Houses lay a babbling invalid, delirious and wasted to a mere skeleton. He was a pitiful victim of malaria and its so-called "cure", rum. In his fevered ravings he began to express his repentance for his sins.

"Great Spirit, give me strength to walk again, if this is Your will," he prayed, doing this as he had been told that white people did.

In a quavering voice and in almost inaudible syllables, he sang some of the sacred songs of his religion, the songs of the spirits, the harvest song, the song of gratitude for the corn. When he stopped for breath, he murmured, "Evil has befallen all of us because of the strong drink; it has laid me low."

That night he slept fitfully, and his needs were supplied by his faithful daughter. Through the night she heard him murmuring as if talking to unseen beings, but before morning he was quiet.

Next day his dimming eyes looked out at the late May sunshine, and he breathed a sigh of gratitude. "The Creator made this sunshine," he said, and then he shut his eyes again.

Soon afterward, while both his daughter and her husband were sitting on the doorstep, they heard him speak as if conversing with someone.

"*Nyuh*," he replied to some inaudible voice, "I'll do it!"

Then they heard him rise from his bed and shuffle toward the door. Quickly the daughter sprang up, but only to see her father totter. She caught his withered form just as he crumpled to the floor. With her husband's help the limp figure was carried back to his rude bed.

The bereft daughter stood upon the doorstep and gave the wail that told of the death of a relative. Neighbours heard the cry and passed the news along.

"Speed your way," said the grieving Yewenot to her husband Hatgwiyot. "Find Cornplanter and Awl Breaker and tell them that Handsome Lake is dead."

In response Awl Breaker, a chief of distinction, came to the lodge of mourning, but Cornplanter, the half brother of Handsome Lake, continued his hoeing until the field was finished.

The house soon filled with sympathizing neighbours, and even the drunken raftsmen sobered up to keep the peace while death lay within a mourner's lodge. After all, Handsome Lake was a sachem; he had been an able adviser.

Awl Breaker, as he looked at the silent form, began to wonder about the strange look on Handsome Lake's face. He seemed to be watching something, perhaps even speaking in his sleeping mind. Awl Breaker bent over the stiffened body and placed his hand over the heart.

"Hold back your wails," he said. "Our sachem is not dead and may rise again. Let us watch and be patient."

Running his hand over the body, Awl Breaker felt the shrunken flesh respond, though few would believe him. How could a skeleton like that be alive? Near relatives continued to mourn, thinking revival impossible.

About noon the watchful Awl Breaker saw the lips of the "dead man" move as if talking. Warm blood was pulsing now in his chest and could be felt at his back. Awl Breaker spoke to the silent figure, asking, "My uncle, have you recovered?"

To the astonishment of everyone the shrouded figure answered, "I believe that I have recovered."

Though manifestly weak, he spoke with seeming assurance, exclaiming, "Never before have I seen such wondrous visions!"

The erstwhile mourners pressed against the walls of the shack and listened. Not another voice interfered.

"First I thought I heard someone speaking," said Handsome Lake. "I thought it was only my sickness, and when asked if I would come to the door, I replied, '*Nyuh!*' Yet the voices seemed very real, and I arose to go to the door. There before me were three men, with a fourth indistinctly behind. These men were in fine, clean raiment, and their faces were painted red, as if it had been done the day before. Never before have I seen such commanding men. In their hands they held bows, carried like canes, and they bore sprigs of huckleberry bushes with berries of all colours."

His eyes were open now, and Handsome Lake turned his head to look at the crowd with eyes that were very bright. He paused and then resumed his account.

"The four beings told me," he testified, "that they had been sent to me by He Who made us. Then they told me to take the berries and eat them as medicine for my restoration."

He proceeded to tell what medicine people he would consult and how one draft of their brew would cause new strength to come to him. The story, as preserved by the Seneca, tells how he took the medicine, how he gained his strength, and how he soon was able to call a council, at which he told of his marvelous visions, all witnessed in the few hours of his unconsciousness.

In a newly vibrant voice, Handsome Lake told of his call to the service of his people and how he had been instructed to give them word of the better way of life.

It was not long after that, that Handsome Lake proclaimed that the Creator had revealed to him the four great offences that lay at the base of all Indian misery. The great offences were strong drink, witchcraft, gambling, and secret poisoning, but reluctance to have children, unfaithfulness to one's mate, fiddle dancing, and card playing were also evil.

Arthur C. Parker

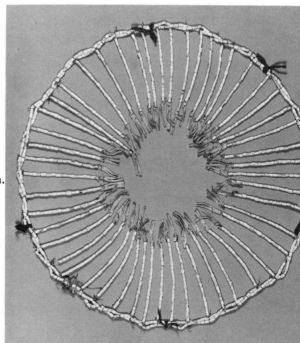

Iroquois wampum.

ON THE DEATH OF AN UNCLE

In the Six Nations the Mohawk, Onondaga, and Seneca are called the elder nations; the Oneida, Cayuga, and Tuscarora the younger nations.

If a chief from one of the elder nations dies, his tribe is consoled by the chiefs of the younger nations who mourn for him as they would for a father or an uncle.

The address of the "younger brothers" is divided into seven parts, each of which has its own wampum string. In making his speech the Orator "reads" each string of wampum.

1(a)   Now — now this day — now I come to your door where you are mourning in great darkness, prostrate with grief. For this reason we have come here to mourn with you. I will enter your door, and come before the ashes, and mourn with you there; and I will speak these words to comfort you.

1(b)   Now our uncle has passed away, he who used to work for all, that they might see the brighter days to come, — for the whole body of warriors and also for the whole body of women, and also the children that were running around, and also for the little ones creeping on the ground, and also those that are tied to the cradle-boards: for all these he used to work that they might see the bright days to come. This we say, we three brothers.

1(c)   Now the ancient lawgivers have declared — our uncles that are gone, and also our elder brothers — they have said, it is worth twenty — it was valued at twenty — and this was the price of the one who is dead. And we put our words on it [i.e. the wampum], and they recall his name — the one that is dead. This we say and do, we three brothers.

1(d)   Now there is another thing we say, we younger brothers. He who has worked for us has gone afar off; and he also will in time take with him all these — the whole body of warriors and also the whole body of women — they will go with him. But it is still harder when the woman shall die, because with her the line is lost. And also the grandchildren and the little ones who are running around — these he will take away; and also those that are creeping on the ground, and also those that are on the cradle-boards; all these he will take away with him.

1(e)   Now then another thing we will say, we three brothers. Now you must feel for us; for we came here of our own goodwill — came to your door that we might say this. And we will say that we will try to do you good. When the grave has been made, we will make it still better. We will adorn it, and cover it with moss. We will do this, we three brothers.

2   Now another thing we will say, we younger brothers. You are mourning in the deep darkness. I will make the sky clear for you, so that you will not see a cloud. And also I will give the sun to shine upon you, so that you can look upon it peacefully when it goes down. You shall see it when it is going. Yea! the sun shall seem to be hanging just over you, and you shall look upon it peacefully as it goes down. Now I have hope that you will yet see the pleasant days. This we say and do, we three brothers.

3   Now then another thing we say, we younger brothers. Now we will open your ears, and also your throat, for there is something that has been choking you and we will also give you the water that shall wash down all the troubles in your throat. We shall hope that after this your mind will recover its cheerfulness. This we say and do, we three brothers.

4   Now then there is another thing we say, we younger brothers. We will now remake the fire, and cause it to burn again. And now you can go out before the people and go on with your duties and your labours for the people. This we say and do, we three brothers.

5   Now also another thing we say, we younger brothers. You must converse with your nephews; and if they say what is good, you must listen to it. Do not cast it aside. And also if the warriors should

say anything that is good, do not reject it. This we say, we three brothers.

6   Now then another thing we say, we younger brothers. If any one should fall — it may be a principal chief will fall and descend into the grave — then the horns shall be left on the grave, and as soon as possible another shall be put in his place. This we say, we three brothers.

7   Now another thing we say, we younger brothers. We will gird the belt on you, with the pouch, and the next death will receive the pouch, whenever you shall know that there is death among us, when the fire is made and the smoke is rising. This we say and do, we three brothers.

Now I have finished. Now show me the man!

FORBIDDEN VOICE

Mrs. Alma Greene (Forbidden Voice) grew up in a big Ontario farm house where chores such as milking, egg gathering, and butter-making were part of every day just as they were part of every day for the white children who lived on the other side of the reserve boundary. But Forbidden Voice, a Mohawk princess, grew up to become a clan mother and many of her childhood experiences were very different from those of her white playmates.

THE HAND

When Forbidden Voice was six, her teenaged brother disappeared overnight. He came back the next day but he was very quiet, and he had a black eye. She pestered him to tell her where he had gone and what had happened and finally he told her. This is what he told her.

He and another boy had decided they hated the long hours of work they had to put in on a farm and wanted to have fun like the boys who had money in their pockets and sneaked into the nearby taverns on weekends. One of these cutups was now in jail, but the boys had decided that even jail was more exciting than their own hard life. So they saved up their pennies and planned to run away.

On the night they chose, they sneaked out of their homes late at night and began walking.

They walked for miles and miles, and after a while a storm blew up. They were still in familiar territory and they knew there was a barn nearby, so they decided to shelter there for the rest of the night. At daylight they would be on their way again, for they had made up their minds to go to some faraway place where there would be no cows to milk or pigs to feed.

They knew people would be out looking for them, so when they got inside the barn they climbed up to the hayloft, took off their shoes, and settled down. Still whispering so they wouldn't be heard and wondering who would be the first to notice their absence, they drifted off to sleep.

Suddenly the other boy jumped up screaming "Help me." He seemed to be struggling with something on his face. Just as the little girl's brother got to him, the boy jerked the something away and threw it as hard as he could.

It flew right back as if it were alive, slapped the brother's face and clung to his cheek. It was an unattached hand. The brother tried to fight it off but it had powerful fingers and it kept hitting his head and face. When he beat it off for a moment if flew to the other boy, and it kept flying from one face to the other till they tumbled down from the loft and ran out of the barn.

They ran all the way home with the hand slapping at them and it

170   I AM AN INDIAN

was broad daylight before they noticed they had left their shoes back at the barn.

THE RIVER OF LIFE

Indians believe in dreams.

When Forbidden Voice was eleven, her mother became very ill with pneumonia.

It was the night of the sixth of January. The family had gone to a Twelfth Night party on the reserve and Forbidden Voice was still full of excitement because there had been a tree with gifts, and a play about Hiawatha written by the minister's daughter, and she had had a part in the play. On the way home her father had tucked her in a blanket and put her in a clothes basket tied to a hand sleigh and pulled her home through the bright night with starlight frosting the snowy trees. When they got home her father had started a fire in the heater and everyone stood around for a while in their wraps until the room was cosy.

Then, about three in the morning, her mother fell ill.

The doctor came in the morning, and every day after that for fourteen days. Then there came a terrible three days when her mother slipped into a coma and the doctor told them to give up hope. When the family left her mother's room at mealtimes, Forbidden Voice would stay there by herself and pray to the Great Spirit to spare her. On the fourth morning her father came and roused Forbidden Voice and told her to come quickly for her mother was dying. When someone in a family dies, everyone must come; no one must be left sleeping. So Forbidden Voice left her bed and rushed to her mother's bedside screaming, "Mother, don't leave me."

At that her mother slowly opened her eyes and looked at her and smiled. "No I will not leave you," she said. "Not for a little while."

Presently she began to talk. She said she had been a long way away. After she had walked a distance she had reached the River of Life. Over the water towards her came a girl, holding out her hand and saying, "Mother I have come to meet you." It was her daughter, one of the five children her parents had lost before Forbidden Voice was born. Her name had been Josephine and she had died at sixteen.

Josephine told the mother not to be afraid, and hand in hand they walked through the water. When they reached the other side, the mother found her clothes were as white as snow and there was great peace in her soul. As they walked on, she saw the houses that mortals prepare for themselves hereafter. One she described was a house made of roses; for each good deed on earth a rose had been added. The air was fragrant with their perfume, and each rose was a beacon of light illuminating the house with rainbow colours. Then the mother asked to see the previous babies she had lost in their infancy. It was then that Josephine said to her, "I cannot take you farther. You will have to go back, for the prayers of my youngest sister, asking that you be spared have been heard in heaven. You must go back for her sake."

The mother turned back. She saw a crowd at a distance and as she drew nearer, she saw it was a funeral procession. It was her coffin and two maidens were walking behind it dressed in deep mourning with black veils almost covering their faces. When they turned she saw they were her two living daughters and then she knew she would live until her daughters were grown women.

A man approached and told her she would come presently to a flock of sheep and one would have a light blue ribbon round its neck. If she could catch this one she would be allowed to stay, but if she could not she would have to return to earth. She walked on and there were the sheep, the one with the blue ribbon standing apart from the rest. She tried to catch it but could not keep her grip. So she walked on.

Then she met the man who had approached her before and he told her that when she reached her home a seamstress would be there with her gown.

If it fit her she could return with the seamstress. When she reached home the seamstress was there and in her hand was a beautiful shimmering blue gown. But when she put it on, the gown had only one sleeve.

And so she went to her bedroom and there were her family around her bed, and she heard Forbidden Voice's despairing cry, "Mother, don't leave me."

THE DOLLS

One Christmas after Forbidden Voice had started to school and was beginning to learn English, she was taken into Brantford on Christmas Eve. There in the street she bumped into two white children from her school, and they were wild with excitement. They could talk of nothing but Santa Claus, who was coming that very night with his magic reindeer and a sackful of toys more splendid than you could imagine.

One of them said she was going to get a new doll, and pointed out the one she wanted in a shop window. It was beautiful. It had shining yellow hair and blue eyes and pretty lace clothes and it was bigger than any doll Forbidden Voice had ever seen, the size of a real baby.

That night when Forbidden Voice came home she was feverish with excitement. "Was Santa Claus going to bring her a lot of brand-new toys, too?" she asked greedily.

Her mother explained gently that Santa Claus was the white man's way of making children happy. "But," she said, "We real people, we Indians, are happy because we have a Creator who created all things to make us so. He dwells in the sun, moon and stars, and in the sunshine and rain that make things grow. That is more than enough, and so we have been told by our ancient forefather always to be happy and thankful."

The little girl picked up her two old cornhusk dolls thoughtfully and carried them to bed, where she was soon fast asleep. That night she had a dream.

She dreamed she saw Santa Claus with a huge pack of toys standing beside the stocking she had hung up. Not wanting to disturb him she closed her eyes, but when she opened them again he was gone and in her stocking was the doll from the store window, except that its face was like the face of one of the little white girls she had talked to in town. Beside the stocking was a doll carriage and also a toy dog. She took the doll and hugged it tightly in her arms. She picked up the toy dog and hugged it too.

Suddenly she heard loud sobs. It was her own dog, Tori, howling pitifully just under her window. Then there was sobbing all around, and when she turned she saw her two cornhusk dolls crying as if their hearts would break.

Then, as she watched, the cornhusk dolls began to move. They jumped to the floor and, with a war cry, began a ceremonial dance. At the same instant, other cornhusk dolls come in swarms like bees, through the cracks of the walls and ceiling and floors, until the room was filled. As they danced to the tom-tom, they trampled the doll carriage to bits. The toy dog dropped from her arms. The beautiful doll with its real-life face began to shrivel. Then, one by one, the cornhusk dolls returned through the cracks they had come by and the room was empty, except for the whimpering of Tori under her window.

When the little girl woke the next morning her two cornhusk dolls were safe beside her on the bed and as she hugged them she vowed that no white man's toy would ever take their place.

Alma Greene

Mrs. Alma Greene and her granddaughter sit behind plastic-foam flowers of Mrs. Greene's own creation.

Chapter IX

People of the Sunrise

Living next to the sun on the eastern edge of "the world", young Wabanaki men in bark canoes had conquered the roaring waves of the Atlantic long before Columbus reached this continent.

From what is now Nova Scotia they paddled north to the island Europeans thought of as "new found land" to raid the Beothuk. They paddled south for trade and war as far as the present state of Rhode Island and perhaps beyond. The five Wabanaki tribes — the Micmac, Malecite, Abnaki, Passamaquoddy, and Penobscot — travelled west as well. During the eighteenth century they sent representatives to Caugnawaga, near Montreal, to renew and confirm their alliance with one another and with the Iroquois.

Before signing this alliance, the Wabanaki shared with their western neighbours, the Huron and Algonkians, a fierce and bitter battle against the Mohawks and other Iroquois. Wars among the tribes and with the immigrant Europeans were fought at a terrible price — by the mid-seventeenth century the mighty Huron nation had been reduced to one small group living at Lorette near Quebec City.

The People of the Sunrise have learned from the European all the techniques of modern living. Some have married Europeans and many have accepted their religion. But the casual observer who assumes that they are no different from their neighbours will be mistaken.

GLUSKAP AND THE KING OF FRANCE

Gluskap, the great transformer, had the power to change the shape of rivers, mountains, and even living creatures.

This story of Gluskap's trip to France is told by the people at King's Clear, New Brunswick.

Once Gluskap saw boats sailing by. He walked out into the sea and picked one up and examined it carefully. He asked the crew who they were and they told him they were subjects of the King of France. This made Gluskap think, and as he went ashore he made up his mind that he should like to see Paris where the King of France lived.

"Grandmother, let us go to France."

"All right, let us go."

As soon as it was decided, Gluskap got some food together, and he and his grandmother went down to the harbour of Saint John and picked out an island for their ship. They put some provisions aboard and made up a crew of squirrels because they were the best climbers around, loosened the island from the bottom, and sailed away.

After a long time they came to Paris and anchored their ship near the King's castle. It was almost dark when they dropped anchor, and the next morning the King looked out his window and saw an island with many tall trees in the harbour. Since the King needed some lumber he gave orders, saying, "Go send some soldiers out to cut down those trees."

Gluskap observed their coming and cried, "Look, Grandmother, the King of France is coming to see us." But the soldiers climbed aboard and started killing the squirrels and cutting down the trees. "What are you doing, cutting down my masts and killing my squirrels?"

"They are trees and squirrels and they belong to the King of France."

Then Gluskap became angry and thought to kill the soldiers, but his grandmother said no, that would not be polite. Gluskap put them in the boats and sent them to the King and told them to tell the monarch that Gluskap and his grandmother had come to see him.

When the King saw his soldiers and found they had not cut the trees, he was very angry. When they told him why, he was even angrier and sent the soldiers to bring Gluskap and his grandmother to him.

"Who are you?" asked the King. "Why don't you let the soldiers cut the trees on my island?"

"I am Gluskap and this is my grandmother, and the island is my boat."

This angered the King, and he ordered his soldiers to shoot Gluskap, but the latter just smiled and smoked his stone pipe and the bullets bounced off. Seeing this, the King realized that he had to think of some better way to dispose of these people, so he called his wise men. They said "Put them in a cannon and shoot it."

The soldiers brought a great cannon and filled it half full of powder, and then shoved in Gluskap and his grandmother, and put a wad on top of them. When everything was ready the soldiers stood around, and somebody told the King, who gave orders to fire it. One man put a match to it and there was a terrible explosion.

After the smoke cleared away they discovered that the gun had blown up, killing a thousand soldiers. On the ground smoking their stone pipes and quite unharmed sat Gluskap and his grandmother. They got up and went down to their ship and sailed back to Saint John, where they anchored and where the ship still remains.

However, Gluskap was so disgusted by his treatment at the hands of the white men that he and his grandmother went away somewhere far to the north where they still live. Before they left they promised the Indians that they would return and drive the white men from the land, when Gluskap had filled his wigwam to the very top with arrowheads, which he is still making.

THE WIZARD AND THE CHRISTIAN PRIEST

Dr. J. D. Prince visited and studied with the Abnaki at the beginning of this century. He noticed that the story-tellers used poetry to tell their tales, and when he translated their stories into English he wrote them as poetry.

THE WIZARD AND THE CHRISTIAN PRIEST

A priest of God came to an Indian town
And settled there to teach the people truth,
Which some received and others spurned with scorn.
Some hostile Mohawks fell upon that town,
Killing the folk, all save the Priest and one,
An Indian of many magic gifts.

Late in the afternoon of that same day
The Mohawks reached their village with these two:
The holy Priest and Wizard skilled in craft.
The Mohawks held a council by the fire
Discussing how to torture best the twain,
So as to see their frenzy, and enjoy
With gloating satisfaction every pain.
They all agreed to heat two earthen pots
On fiery coals unto the whitest heat;
Then place these pots upon the head of each
And watch them dance about till life was spent.

With merry whoop they started up the fires;
Began at once to heat the torture pots.
Soon, when they thought the glow was great enough,
They first of all laid hands upon the Priest.
Then he who had been taken with the Priest
At once brought all his magic arts to bear,
And burst his bonds asunder with a yell

That curdled every heart among the foe.
The Wizard cried in Indian tongue. *"Nda
Awâni niûna ndelima —
Magahôûana,"* which means: "My friends,
We shall not torture any one (to-day)."
And then he leapt upon the fiery coals
And danced and danced, until his feet did fry
And sizzle hot like bacon in a pan.
Then all the Indians were full of fear.
But when to crown the horror of the whole
They saw the wizard put the glowing pot
On his own head and leap about in glee,
They all took flight in terror to the woods.
Then spake the Wizard: "Father, now escape."

When they had reached all safe and sound their home,
The priest said to the Wizard: "O my son,
Thou shouldst repent and turn thee from thine art
Unto God's ways and ever keep the Faith."
Then quoth the Wizard laughing: "Father mine,
Had I repented and mine art eschewed,
Then were we both of us dead men this day."

J. D. Prince

Indian fishing camp, Restigouche, N.B.

THE MAKING OF THE GREAT LAW

All the Wabanaki tribes formed a federation with the Iroquois nations in order to put an end to the wars which had killed so many of their people.

The Passamaquoddy have preserved in their wampum records the story of the founding of this alliance which is hundreds of years old.

Many bloody battles had been fought, many men, women, and children had been tortured by constant and cruel wars, when some of the wise men began to think that something must be done, and done quickly. They accordingly sent messengers to all parts of the country, some going to the South, others to the East, and others to the

West and Northwest. Some even went as far as the Wabanaki. It was many moons before the messengers reached the farthest tribes.

When they arrived at each nation, they notified the people that the powerful tribes of the Iroquois had sent them to announce the tidings of a great council for a treaty of peace. Every Indian who heard the news rejoiced, for all were weary of the never-ending wars. Every tribe sent two or more of their wisest men as representatives to the great council.

When all the delegates had assembled, they began to discuss what was best to do. All of them seemed tired of their evil lives.

The leading chief addressed the council in these words: "As we look back upon our blood-stained trail, we see that many wrongs have been done by all our people. Our bloody tomahawks, clubs, bows, and arrows must be buried. They must be buried for all time."

The council decided to make a general treaty of peace, a treaty of peace between all the nations there gathered together. And they set a day when the ceremonies should begin. For seven suns a strict silence was observed, during which each delegate meditated on the speech he should make to the council. Each person also tried to discover, in his own mind, the best means for avoiding wars. These days were called the Wigwam of Silence.

After seven days, they held another wigwam, which was called the Wigwam of Oratory. Each delegate made a speech in which he related the history of his nation. He told about all the hardships and cruelties that his people had suffered during the wars. Each speaker ended his address with words like these: "The time has now come when we must think about our women and our children, our crippled men and our old warriors. We must have pity on them, for they have suffered equally with our strongest and bravest warriors."

When all the speeches had been delivered, the council decided to erect an extensive fence, and within the fence to build a large wigwam. In this wigwam they would build a big fire. They would have a whip made and would place it in the hand of a father who would be the guard of the large wigwam. If any person did wrong, the father would punish him with the whip. Every person within the fence must obey all the orders of the father, who would be not only guard but also fire-keeper. It would be his duty to see that the fire in the wigwam never went out.

The fence symbolized a treaty of peace for all the Indian nations that took part in the council. There were fourteen of these nations, in which there were many tribes. All these were to go within the fence and dwell there. If any should do wrong, he would be liable for punishment with the whip at the hands of the father.

The wigwam within the fence symbolized a universal house of all the tribes, in which they might live in peace, without disputes and quarrels. They would be like members of a family.

The big fire in the wigwam symbolized the warmth of the brotherly love developed in the people by the treaty. The father ruling the wigwam and keeping the fire always burning was the Great Chief who lived at Caughnawaga. The whip in his hand represented the Wampum Laws. Disobedience to them was punishable by the consent of all the tribes mentioned in the Great Treaty.

After the Council had drawn up the Great Law and had it recorded in wampum, they made lesser laws and had them recorded also. Every feast, every ceremony, had its own law, its own ritual preserved in the wampum.

"All these records are to be read aloud, in every tribe, from time to time," the council decreed. "If this is done, the peace that we have made will endure forever."

The council also made boundaries around the hunting grounds, so that each tribe knew where it could hunt without being attacked by another tribe.

In former days, the members of the Wabanaki nation and the members of the Iroquois Six Nations had waged bloody and unceasing war with one another. But after the meeting of the Great Council, after the making of the Great Law, the Wabanaki lived as one nation, at peace with all the Iroquois tribes. There was no strife within the nation, and there was no war with their neighbours. All presented a united front for peace.

NOW I AM LEFT

Jealousy and rivalry in love are not new inventions, but in the old days getting the best of your rival might mean taking drastic steps. This translation of such a rivalry was made by John Reade, who worked with the Wabanaki around 1880.

Now I Am Left

Now I am left on this lonely island to die —
No one to hear the sound of my voice.
Who will bury me when I die?
Who will sing my death-song for me?
My false friends leave me here to die alone;
Like a wild beast, I am left on this island to die.
I wish the wind spirit would carry my cry to my love!
My love is as swift as the deer; he would speed through the forest
    to find me;
Now I am left on this lonely island to die.
I wish the spirit of air would carry my breath to my love.
My love's canoe, like the sunlight, would shoot through the water to
    my side;
But I am left on this lonely island to die, with no one to pity me but
    the little birds.
My love is brave and strong; but, when he hears my fate, his stout
    heart will break;
And I am on this lonely island to die.
Now the night comes on, and all is silent but the owl.
He sings a mournful song to his mate, in pity for me.
I will try to sleep.
I wish the night spirit to hear my song; he will tell my love of my
    fate; and when I awake, I shall see the one I love.
I am on this lonely island to die.

THE REVENGE OF THE CARIBOU

The Malecites of New Brunswick share with other North Americans a great respect for the careful hunter who only kills what he needs. The man who is wasteful may invite great misfortune.

In the following story Jim Paul tells about his father who, until this particular episode took place, was a most successful caribou hunter.

One day, while out hunting on a barren near the Salmon river, my father came upon some caribou. As he was still-hunting he crept up as close as he could and then fired at the largest. The animal fell, and, thinking it was mortally wounded, he reloaded to fire at another. However, by the time he had reloaded, he noticed that the animal had risen to its feet, so he fired at it again and it fell once more. On reloading a second time, much to his amazement he observed that it was again standing up. He fired another shot and it fell the third time. He did not attempt to reload as all the other animals had fled; but, drawing his knife, he went up to skin the animal. He cut its throat and then turned it over on its back to cut it up and take out the viscera. Just as the knife touched the animal's heart, it kicked and jumped to its feet. In so doing it knocked the knife out of his hand, cutting him badly between his index finger and his thumb. The caribou jumped to one side and stood staring at him, with eyes as red as blood. The Indian knew at once that some great misfortune had come upon him, so he began running away. As soon as he started the animal began to chase him, but had not gone far before it fell down as if dead. However, the Indian knew that he must not go near it, and continued running until he got back to camp. His companion at once inquired how he had cut his hand, whereupon he told him everything. His companion was not greatly impressed with his misfortune and tried to cheer him up, telling him that he would go back the next morning, skin the animal, and bring its carcass back to camp.

Accordingly, the next morning they started off, but on arriving at the place they found that the animal had disappeared, although some of its intestines were still lying about. "Some great misfortune will surely come on either you or some member of your family," his companion said; and my father replied, "In my youth when I used to hunt north of the St. Lawrence, I killed many more caribou than I could possibly use. Now retribution has come upon me because of it. I will never kill any caribou or eat any caribou meat, or use anything made of caribou skin as long as I live."

On his way back to the camp the trigger of his gun caught in a twig, causing it to be accidently discharged, and narrowly missing his companion. Both of them were so overwhelmed by a sense of impending danger that they packed up and went home. Although no great calamity ever came upon him, he kept his vow so strictly that he never even wore snowshoes with caribou filling; but his luck was never again as good as it had been before.

Jim Paul

Caribou, also called wild reindeer, roam in large herds across northern Canada.

PASSAMAQUODDY WAR SONG

Most scholars agree that the practice of taking scalps was intro-duced by Europeans and is still known as "kinjamus" among the Penobscot after King James, the man who, in their opinion, started the idea. In 1700 a royal bounty of four hundred pounds a scalp (about $5,000 in today's money) ensured the popularity of this new prac-tice among both Indians and non-Indians. This song in which the taking of a scalp has taken on even more significance was collected by J. Walter Fewkes in the late 1800's.

PASSAMAQUODDY WAR SONG

I will arise with my tomahawk in my hand, and I must have revenge
    on that nation which has slain my poor people.
I arise with war club in my hand, and follow the bloody track of
    that nation which killed my people.
I will sacrifice my own life and the lives of my warriors.
I arise with war club in my hand, and follow the track of my enemy.
When I overtake him I will take his scalp and string it on a long
    pole, and I will stick it in the ground, and my warriors will dance
    around it for many days; then I will sing my song for the
    victory over my enemy.

THE FLOATING ISLAND

Nobody knows just when the first white man landed on the Wa-banaki coast, but the Micmac girl who had this particular dream saw a priest as well as sailors. The men who came on her "floating island" came to stay.

When there were no people in this country but Indians, before white people were known, a young woman had a strange dream. She dreamed that a small island came floating in toward the land. On the island were tall trees and living beings. Among them was a man dressed in garments made of rabbit skins.

In those days it was the custom, when anyone had an unusual dream, to consult the wise men of the tribe, especially the prophets and magicians. So the girl related her dream and asked what it meant. The wise men pondered but could make nothing of it. On the second day after the girl's dream, however, something happened that explained it.

When they got up that morning, they saw what seemed to be a small island that had drifted near to the land and become fixed there. There were trees on the island, and what seemed to be a number of bears were crawling about on the branches.

All the Micmac men seized their bows and arrows and spears, and rushed down to the shore to shoot the bears. But they stopped in surprise when they saw that the creatures were not bears but men. And what had seemed to be a small island with trees was really a large boat with long poles rising above it. While the Indians stood watching, some of the men on the ship lowered a strangely built canoe into the water. Several of them jumped into it and paddled ashore.

Among those in the strange canoe was a man dressed in white. As he came toward the shore, he made signs of friendship, by raising his hand toward heaven. He talked to the Indians in an earnest manner, in a language they did not understand.

Now people began to question the girl about her dream.

Lone Cloud, Chief Medical Man of the Micmacs, Nova Scotia, 1928.

"Was it an island like this that you saw in your dream?"

"Yes."

"Is the man in the 'white robe the one you saw in your dream?"

"Yes, he was."

Then some of the prophets and the magicians were greatly displeased — displeased because the coming of these strangers to their land had been revealed to a young girl instead of to them. If an enemy had been about to make an attack upon them, they could have foreseen it and foretold it by the power of their magic. But of the coming of this white-robed man, who proved to be a priest of a new religion, they knew nothing.

The new teacher gradually won his way into their favour, though the magicians opposed him. The people received his instruction and were baptized. The priest learned their language and gave them the prayer-book written in ornamental mark-writing.

WOLVERINE AND THE GREAT SERPENT

The Huron have been Christians for hundreds of years. In this leg-end from Lorette the hero, Wolverine, takes his empty whiskey jug to a tree where one of his more saintly friends had seen the Virgin Mary.

Casting the livid light of his own eyes upon Wolverine, the Great Serpent roared like thunder. He said:

"I hate the Huron race, because it was baptized. I curse it. But I love you, Wolverine, for you are my friend. And I bless you."

"Thanks!" answered Otsatut, his teeth chattering in his mouth. "I am not deaf. Please make your voice not quite so loud. Stand away that I may see you better. Who are you — a dream or a thing of flesh and blood?"

"I am your people's guardian spirit, their first master. Your an-cesters were pagans; they did not know God, only me. The lightning is the flash from my eyelids when they open; the storm is my breath. When I am angry, my voice is the thunder. I tear up the lakes as I go by, and I dig up rivers. Look at the trench there, where I fell; it has turned into a waterfall. And the river below is the trail I left as I passed."

"You are a guardian spirit, a mighty spirit. Can you not do some-thing for me?"

"I can."

"Then lower your voice, please."

The Great Serpent scaled his voice down to a whisper, then chang-ed it into a song like a bird's.

Wolverine said:

"The blackrobe says that you, the guardian spirit of our forefath-ers, and the Devil are one, that you hunt for human souls over the earth. It was not to meet you that I came here, tonight, but to see the white Lady at the Tree of Dreams."

"You are not the blackrobe's son, Wolverine, nor is the Virgin your own patron saint. What were you really looking for?"

Wolverine could only look at the empty jug lying at his feet.

"Enemy of the Christians though am I," said the monster, "I am gentle to my friends. And I love you, Wolverine, I will shower blessings upon you."

Reassured, Wolverine thought that the Tree of Dreams was not such a disappointment after all. He raised his jug from the ground and in smiling expectation held it forward in his hands.

As the Great Serpent coiled his way towards him, Wolverine tried to hide behind the tree.

"You frighten me," he said in a quavering voice.

"I am your friend," murmured the monster.

"Why then remain a serpent?"

"If you prefer it, I can change you, Otsatut, into a toad, a bullfrog, or a lizard."

"You are much too kind. I would rather stay as I was born. Could you not change yourself into something less frightful?"

The Serpent answered:

"Yes, I can be a wolf, a white bear, a puma, or a rattlesnake. I can even make myself into a man."

"Be a man then, so that we can talk."

The monster vanished, then reappeared in the form of a puff of white smoke on the riverbank. Out of the smoke stepped a dwarf with eyes sparkling like a puma's and a wicked smile curling his lips.

"Well, now," said the dwarf.

"Now I can talk to you," said Wolverine, quite at ease.

At last he would get all the firewater he needed, enough to last him for a lifetime. He and his friends could drink their fill.

The dwarf snorted so fiercely through one of his nostrils that the empty jug was blown away. He then turned to Wolverine with a scowl and said:

"You are a lazy dunce, you won't work for your living."

"Why should I work?" countered the Indian.

"And you expect to win a treasure . . ."

"Go on, go on! You too preach to me like the blackrobe. The Devil is not what I had thought. He too would have me save my son!"

"You may live to find it out. Meanwhile, here is a purse of gold. It is a witch purse. Tie it to your belt; it is yours for a lifetime. It will never be empty."

"You are a great chief!" said Wolverine.

"Be silent! You are vain and foolish. Gladly would you don the costume of a nobleman yourself, and strut about in cocked hat and plume. Yet you have not enough to cover your nakedness."

"Preaching again!"

"Well then, here are silks and satins, here is purple wampum in bands for your belt, and strings of white wampum for your neck; silver bands for your arms, and bracelets for your wrists."

Wolverine could not hide his joy. "Like a chief I shall call upon Ononthio, who governs Canada."

"Yes, call upon him," agreed the dwarf with a smirk. And Wolverine sank his hands deep into the rustling finery.

"You are a drunkard; a riverful would never quench your thirst. Here is a bottle for you! It never empties however much you may pour from it."

"It is magic!" Wolverine exclaimed, and his hands eagerly shot forward to grasp the flask.

"It is yours for eternity."

"Truly you are a great spirit!"

"The head chief refused to give you his daughter to wife, for you are lazy, poor, and a rake. But as soon as he hears the sound of gold in this purse, he will change his mind."

"He must change his mind!"

"The blackrobe wants to throw you out of the village. He does not know whom he has to deal with. Now you are powerful for I shall protect you. I have in mind to send weasels to his roof and rats to his pantry, to plague him. Every night I shall call all the tomcats of the village to his roof, and he will no longer be able to sleep the sleep of the just."

Wolverine danced about gleefully as the dwarf was still speaking. "But tell me, what do you want in exchange for all your gifts?"

A wicked smile played at the corner of the dwarf's mouth as he left Wolverine puzzling for an answer.

"What do you want for your gifts?" Wolverine again asked the dwarf, tugging at the strings of his witch purse.

"Are you so rich that you cannot make a choice?" answered the dwarf.

"The payment is just a trifle, a thing you cannot dispose of to anyone but me."

"What is it? A vow to drink myself to death?"

"Try to think. Have you nothing else to offer in exchange?"

"Nothing — except my soul. Surely you cannot want my soul?"

The dwarf nodded.

"But where shall I sleep, the night after my death?"

"In my own heaven, good Wolverine. And you shall need no blanket there."

"I may be thirsty. Is there any firewater in your heaven?"

"But you have the bottle that never empties. It is yours forever."

"And shall I make merry with other drinkers?"

"My friend, you shall. It will be one long carouse."

"What a jolly place!"

The dwarf rubbed his spidery finger against his nose.

"There is just one little thing more. Should you reform someday by repenting your sins, remember that our bargain still holds good."

Wolverine would let the future take care of itself. For the present he thought only of the purse and the bottle.

Before parting with him, the dwarf still had one more word to say. But Wolverine no longer listened.

Wolverine's vision under the Tree of Dreams had come to an end. Dazed, he went back home that night, and awakened, a new man, the next morning.

What about the purse and the magic bottle?

They were there, in his lap, and that was the worst that could happen to him and to his tribe.

From that day Wolverine was the wealthiest man in the country, and a real live devil. He gave sagamite feasts eight days long. Rum flowed as if out of a spring, and lust followed in its wake. The old folk gossiped, as they often do. They whispered that Wolverine had dug up a treasure, that he was a spy in British pay, that he fished with two lines in muddy water, or that he had sold his soul to the devil. All this chatter was of no importance while the fun lasted — many years.

The missionaries could never stop the Lorette orgies. Brightly uniformed officers used to come from Quebec and hold court at Wolverine's. They would not go back to town until they had lost their cocked hat and their fine feathers. That is how a few of their names, white men's names, became the property of Lorette families.

The British officers were fond of Lorette, just like the French, and they were always welcome. Big guns were fired in their honour, they were made high chiefs, Indian names were bestowed upon them. The-Dawn-of-Day, Crimson-Sky, and He-Sails-on-the-Sky. But that is now a thing of the past.

What happened to Wolverine in the end is of little consequence. The end of the story is never told. Perhaps it has no ending. What is left for all to remember is that the Great Serpent remained under the waterfalls for a hundred years or more, until the Jesuit missionaries decided to expel him.

From an old Huron legend as told to Marius Barbeau

Alanais Obomsowin (Abnaki), famous folk singer, talks with Marius Barbeau at the National Museum in Ottawa, 1969.

N'JACQUES AND KITTY

Today there are a whole series of Euro-American stories which the Wabanaki enjoy perhaps even more than Gluskap stories. N'Jacques or Little Jack has a European origin but the stories about him belong to the people, their way of living, and their sense of humour. Some are more traditional and local and some like "N'Jacques and Kitty" have an international flavour.

Once at Carlisle, in Pennsylvania, there was an Indian from Old Town named Jack. He was homesick and wanted very much to go home but he had no money. Despite this fact he started out on foot. He had not gone very far when a farmer picked him up in his wagon and took him along. He offered Jack work at nine dollars a week picking apples, room and board included. Jack accepted.

After the apple picking was over, the farmer told Jack he could no longer keep him, but that there was a brewery eight miles away where he could get work if he went there the next morning.

The farmer left that day, and the next morning Jack asked the farmer's wife if he could borrow the horse and wagon to go to the brewery. The farmer's wife liked Jack and said he could have the beast. He could "steal her for the day," but he was to remember that the farmer thought more of Kitty [for that was the horse's name] than he did of his wife and, therefore, Jack was to take good care of her. She did not know what the farmer would do if anything happened to the mare.

Jack said he would be very careful and then harnessed Kitty and drove to the brewery. When he reached his destination, he found the road closed by a gate, which he opened, and he drove on up to the building. Leaving Kitty on a "ground hitch" he went to see the brewer. Upon his return he found the mare down beside a pile of malt, her mouth covered with foam. The animal made no movement, although Jack kicked and pounded her. Thinking her dead, Jack tried to blame the brewer, but the brewer said it was Jack's fault for bringing her past the gate. Now the beast was dead on his land.

"Skin her, pull off her shoes, and sell them. That way you can get enough money to have someone haul her out of here," said the brewer.

Jack felt very badly about poor Kitty, but he got out his knife and skinned her from nose to tail. (This is the way the Indians always skin important animals such as bears. Lesser creatures are skinned tail to nose.) He pulled off her shoes and threw the shoes and the hide into the cart along with the harness. Then he got between the shafts and dragged the wagon home, hung the skin in the barn, put the wagon away, and went up to his room.

A little later the farmer came home. First, he asked if the chores were done, and his wife said they were. Then, "Did you tend to Kitty?"

"No. You'll have to ask Jack. He's upstairs."

Jack said, "Kitty's taken care of."

The next morning the farmer went into the barn, but he could not find Kitty. He called Jack, and Jack told the truth. The farmer said that he would have to work on the farm until the horse was paid for, and Jack agreed to it. Just then they heard a whinny outside the barn. "Look out the door. Somebody's horse has broken loose. We must catch it and take it home." Jack looked and there was Kitty. She had gotten drunk on the malt and Jack had skinned her while she was unconscious.

"Quick, Jack! Run to the stream and cut some willow pegs. They're good for healing. We'll put her skin back on, peg it together, and put her in the south pasture. Maybe she'll get well." Jack did as he was told, happy to think he might not have to pay for the mare after all.

They put her in the south pasture with her skin pegged on and left her. About a month later they went down to see how the creature was getting on. They looked but could not find Kitty. Then they looked behind them and saw a bunch of bushes following them. It was Kitty. The willow pegs had sprouted and turned to bushes. "Well," said Jack, "now when you want firewood all you have to do is drive Kitty up to the kitchen and cut what you need."

Later Jack persuaded the farmer to sell Kitty to a circus, and they made enough money so Jack could go back to Old Town on his share of the profits.

EPILOGUE

DRUMS OF MY FATHER

A hundred thousand years have passed
Yet, I hear the distant beat of my father's drums
I hear his drums throughout the land
His beat I feel within my heart.

The drums shall beat, so my heart shall beat,
And I shall live a hundred thousand years.

Shirley Daniels
(Ojibway)

This book is printed on 60 lb. Belvedere Opaque in
11/13 Times Roman with 18 point and 30 point Perpetua light
italic headings.
5 6 7 8 9 10 Dey 78 77 76 75 74

Printed and bound in Canada